Delivering WOW

Delivering WOW

HOW DENTISTS CAN BUILD A **FASCINATING BRAND** AND ACHIEVE MORE WHILE **WORKING LESS**

Dr. ANISSA HOLMES

NEW YORK

LONDON • NASHVILLE • MELBOURNE • VANCOUVER

Delivering WOW

HOW DENTISTS CAN BUILD A **FASCINATING BRAND** AND ACHIEVE MORE WHILE **WORKING LESS**

© 2019 Dr. ANISSA HOLMES

Published in New York, New York, by Morgan James Publishing. Morgan James is a trademark of Morgan James, LLC. www.MorganJamesPublishing.com

ISBN 978-1-68350-977-6 paperback
ISBN 978-1-68350-978-3 eBook
Library of Congress Control Number: 2018934764

Cover Design by:
Rachel Lopez
www.r2cdesign.com

Interior Design by:
Bonnie Bushman
The Whole Caboodle Graphic Design

Morgan James is a proud partner of Habitat for Humanity Peninsula and Greater Williamsburg. Partners in building since 2006.

Get involved today! Visit
www.MorganJamesBuilds.com

Table of Contents

Foreword

Worldwide, there are nearly two million dentists, and each day we go to work to do two things, but only one of those is something we actually learned in school. What did we learn in school? How to practice dentistry. What's the other thing, the one that all those years of school never really prepared us for? How to run a business! And after running a practice for thirty years, I maintain that it is an entirely different animal than the regular small business.

As the publisher of *Dentaltown* Magazine and the founder of Dentaltown.com, I have been blessed with meeting thousands of dentists. I can't think of one who has grown a practice as quickly and successfully as Dr. Anissa Holmes. She was voted one of the top twenty-five women in dentistry, and frankly, I think she is one of the top 25 *people* in dentistry, period.

The fact is, the business of dentistry is a world unto itself. There are so few quality resources out there for us, which is part of what makes Dr. Holmes' *Delivering WOW: How Dentists Can Build a Fascinating Brand and Achieve More, While Working Less!* such a gem. The vast majority of business books are either a broad overview or a narrowed discussion, which leave you wanting more information, or with the need for five more books on the topics the first didn't bother to address.

Somehow, Dr. Holmes has packed everything from social media and branding to team building and ROI—and more—into an easy read. It takes a dentist to know what another dentist would appreciate, and I for one appreciate a book that reads more like fun—while still teaching me a ton—than another pseudo-textbook that makes me want to tear my eyes out.

One of the hardest aspects of the business of dentistry is that being a dentist is a lot like being a satellite. There might be thousands of us up in orbit at the same time, but we are flying solo and doing our best not to crash and burn. Every once in a while, though, this great profession of ours is graced with someone who not only has mastered the business of dentistry, but one who chooses to share their experience and their knowledge with the rest of us.

Here's what you're going to find in *Delivering WOW: How Dentists Can Build a Fascinating Brand and Achieve More, While Working Less!* that you're not going to find anywhere else. Dr. Holmes does something that few business authors do, and the fact that she does it as it relates to the business of dentistry is phenomenal. Holmes delivers more than the theoretical foundations and principles of running a good business. She lays out the practical—and even literal—steps for the importance of working not just *in* their practice but working *on* their practice. She is a smart businesswoman and dentist who is doing more than sharing her experience and her success. She is laying out how every dentist can achieve extraordinary results in every facet of their practice.

In the first section of this book, you'll be challenged to face whether you have a strong vision for your practice, but more than that, a clear vision for how you approach your business as a whole. Dr. Holmes' clear and concise step-by-step on how to get in there and take action covers everything from developing a thriving company culture and creating everyday systems to keeping the business growing, and—my personal favorite—establishing a brand. Let's not forget that Dr. Holmes is teaching what she's already mastered. After all, she has brilliantly figured out how to master social media with a following of over 50,000 Facebook fans.

If there's one thing above all else that Dr. Holmes does incredibly well in *Delivering WOW: How Dentists Can Build a Fascinating Brand and Achieve More, While Working Less!* it's giving the topic of leadership an evidence-based discussion. You are the CEO of your practice and at the forefront of every major decision in and around it, but leadership wasn't a class in dental school, and you're not going to find any CE courses on it, either. This is what makes Holmes and her book so invaluable. Page after page, she is able to lay out how to develop leadership skills as a dentist and as a business owner. To do one or the other is impressive enough, but to do both at the same time makes this book worth its weight in gold. The sections on building and maintaining an engaged team are especially eye-opening.

Dr. Holmes' passion for helping dentists is something near and dear to my heart. The whole reason I started Dentaltown.com was so that no dentist would ever have to practice alone, and to see this rock star come out with such a solid guide—on top of already giving the dental profession her time as a speaker, podcaster, and clinician—is proof that a dentist can achieve overwhelming success and still have the time and energy to engage in her profession in a tremendous way.

I hope you enjoy *Delivering WOW: How Dentists Can Build a Fascinating Brand and Achieve More While Working Less!* as much as I have.

—**Howard Farran**, DDS, MBA, Founder of Dentaltown.com, and CEO and publisher of *Dentaltown* Magazine Best-selling author of *Uncomplicate Business: All It Takes Is People, Time, and Money*

PREFACE TO THE

Second Edition

In the time since I published the first edition of *Delivering WOW: How Dentists Can Build a Fascinating Brand and Achieve More While Working Less!*, I've helped thousands of dentists improve their practices by applying the principles in the first edition and additional techniques that I teach in my 21-Day Marketing and Practice Growth Challenges and the Delivering WOW Platinum Coaching Program, a premier coaching program full of courses, a private forum, resources, and coaching from the leading experts in the dental industry.

I've been a practicing dentist and entrepreneur since 1999, and I've never been more excited about the future of the dental industry than I am today. In this second edition, I've updated and expanded the lessons from the first edition and added additional strategies for building your practice! These changes and additions reflect the latest strategies in marketing, business, and dental-industry-specific methods for increasing your practice's profitability and operating your practice so it can run without you! I'll also share examples from students in my 21-Day Marketing and Practice Growth Challenges and the Delivering WOW Platinum Coaching Program, as well as my own practice, to show you how our fellow dentists are using these techniques in their practice, so you can make your practice extraordinary.

For me, the first twelve years of my practice were relatively uneventful. Like many dentists, I had a decent business, a supportive team, and very satisfied patients. The problem was I had been just going through the motions for years. In 2011, I walked into my practice and told my team of three that I had a *big* vision. I wanted to grow. I wanted to make a greater impact on people's lives than what we had been making. I wanted to be different. I wanted to create an extraordinary customer experience for my patients. I wanted more!

I knew that doing the same old thing would give me the same results, and I didn't want the same results for me, my family, my team, or my patients. I also knew how important it was to continually learn, have great mentors, and mastermind with people who would hold me accountable, so I hired a coach to help me. My coach reinforced the importance of constant learning, which I had already been committed to. He also emphasized the significance of knowing my numbers and the benefits of creating systems so that the business could run without me.

I implemented these business strategies into my dental practice and "WOW!" my team became inspired. My new-patient numbers increased tenfold, from fifteen to 150. I built a new state-of-the-art office out of profits. I achieved a massive Facebook following of over 50,000 fans. And my practice revenue increased by 300%!

By late 2014, I had achieved my *big* vision and understood the secrets of success. I knew how to "Deliver WOW" to our patients so they would become raving fans and refer their family and friends to me. My life was changed. My family's lives were changed. My team members' lives were changed. And my patients' lives were changed. I couldn't keep those success secrets to myself, so I set another goal—to share what I had learned with dentists around the world to help them Deliver WOW and build better practices, too.

I released the Delivering WOW Dental Podcast the first week of 2016 and reached the first page of iTunes New and Noteworthy for Medicine, Education, Business, and Health. Within the first month, the podcast was being listened to in more than forty countries. Later that year, I released the first edition of this book, *Delivering WOW: How Dentists Can Build a Fascinating Brand and Achieve More, While Working Less!*

Later that year, I also started hosting my Business Acceleration Bootcamps and launched which evolved into 21-Day Marketing and Practice Growth Challenges where I help practices achieve tremendous progress in just three short weeks by focusing on the power of learning and taking action in small bits. Helping practices make so much progress in such a short period of time has been tremendously rewarding for practice leaders and me. You can join other practice leaders making big strides in their practices in our next 21-Day Marketing and Practice Growth Challenge at DeliveringWOWChallenge.com. You'll get twenty-one days of missions, coaching, step-by-step guidance, and more. This is what one practice leader told us about her experience: "This challenge has been so transformational in so many ways! I am so happy to be part of this amazing group. We implemented the whiteboard yesterday for the first time and doubled our production that day. The future looks so bright!"

I also launched a program that would grow into the Delivering WOW Platinum Coaching Program, where leading experts in the dental community and I help dentists improve every facet of their practice I help dentists improve every facet of their practice, including social media tactics, team building, marketing and promotion, and even how to simplify sophisticated marketing tactics like dental-marketing funnels that allow you to onboard new patients while you sleep, and more! I give you all the tools you need to build a WOW practice that helps you make more while working less, including templates, forms, social media images, and even discounts with vendors to make and save you money. We even have options for you to hire my team to implement the tactics we teach. We continue to add more lessons, marketing assets, and discounted services as we continue research, develop, and build new relationships to help you build a better practice in less time.

In this second edition of the *Delivering WOW!* I've completely revamped, updated, and expanded the content that started this all to share the best and latest ways for you to grow your dental practice.

Between the book, podcast, Facebook bootcamps, Facebook group, 21-day challenges, and the Delivering WOW Platinum Coaching Program, thousands of dentists have improved their business and personal lives by implementing Delivering WOW principles and procedures in their practices. I'm excited about the impact this newly updated and expanded book can have for you, too!

Acknowledgments

This book would not have been possible without the help and support of many other people.

Thank you to my husband, Dr. Pierre-John Holmes, whose love and support has been instrumental in helping me pursue my "why" of making a greater impact and helping other dentists Deliver WOW.

Thank you to Ana and Brady for your love and inspiration. You always make me proud.

Thank you to my team at Jamaica Cosmetic Dental Services for your passion and Delivering WOW experiences to each and every patient we serve. Your commitment to learning and growing personally and professionally helps us achieve all of our goals together while developing best practices to help other dentists do the same.

Thank you to my team at DeliveringWOW.com for your commitment to providing the best community, training, and resources for dentists to build WOW practices.

Thank you, too, Nick Pavlidis and Jennifer Harshman, for helping me organize all the latest strategies for building, operating, and marketing dental practices into this updated and expanded edition.

Finally, thank you to my publisher Morgan James for having faith in me and investing in my mission to help dentists Deliver WOW and build stronger practices.

Introduction

Dentists are under increasingly higher stress today. The constant anxiety of student loans and high overhead and the pressure of running a business are even running some out of the profession altogether.

There must be a better way. There *is* a better way.

I wrote this book because I found that better way and want to share it with you. I believe we as dentists can build more profitable and even thriving practices if we take the focus away from doing business as we have always done. This means admitting to ourselves (as well as to our teams) that we might not *have* all the answers right now, but we can find the answers we shift our mindset, look carefully at our leadership, and take action to dream, plan, and take action.

Many people in our profession and other small businesses falsely believe we need to work hard for decades before we can have experience the success and freedom we dreamed of having when we started. They believe the only way to succeed is a slow and steady crawl.

But that simply does not have to be the case. It's a myth.

The truth is you can quickly build a practice of your dreams. All you need to do is decide what that means to you, surround yourself with the right people to help you, and develop and implement a plan to achieve your vision. This book will help you do that.

After reading this, you'll be able to create a clear vision for your practice and your personal life, you'll better understand what it takes to turn your patients into loyal *raving fans*, and you'll have everything you need to create an action plan to achieve your success. You'll be ready to Deliver WOW!

If you want to achieve more while working less, you're in the right place. If you struggle building a winning team, you're in the right place. If you've tried everything you can think of to grow new patient numbers but still can't grow, you're in the right place. If you constantly fail to get patients to accept treatment they need, you're in the right place. If you want to learn how to build a fascinating brand and use Facebook and other social media platforms to make more money, you're in the right place. And if you're tired of feeling guilty, stressed out, or frustrated trying to juggle too much work in too little time while you make too little money, you're in the right place. This book was created, updated, and expanded specifically to help you by sharing even more strategies you can use to build the practice of your dreams. I also share stories from students and clients of mine who have successfully built Delivering WOW practices of their own.

Are you ready?

It's time to create a new reality.

CHAPTER 1

Burnout Versus Balance

r. Scott leans forward and looks into her patient's mouth as she prepares the tooth for a crown. It's a routine procedure she's done many times, but she can practically *feel* the stress and anxiety radiating from her patient, who, at the last minute, grasps her hand to stop her.

"Will it hurt, Doctor?" the patient asks, staring intently at Dr. Scott's face.

Dr. Scott gives the patient a reassuring smile. "No, it will not hurt," she says, straightening up and freeing her hand from her patient's grip. Dr. Scott has explained the procedure already but takes more time to explain it again as she tries to ease her patient's anxiety. After a smattering of additional questions—all of which were answered earlier in an appointment—Dr. Scott's ready to move forward, when Marie, her receptionist, walks into the tiny room, smiling politely at the patient.

Marie whispers into Dr. Scott's ear, whose heart immediately sinks. The next patient is waiting and getting restless, threatening to leave if she isn't seen right away. Dr. Scott quickly glances at her watch. She's been behind all day, since the first patient walked in late and the second appointment took longer than it should have. Every appointment since then has started late, and she hasn't been able to catch up. With this patient's high anxiety, Dr. Scott knows this appointment also will run over.

Dr. Scott had hoped to take a lunch break but knows it will be impossible, as is often the case. In addition to the patient who is waiting and threatening to leave, she has agreed to squeeze in a patient for an emergency visit.

Her lower back is throbbing and sweat is beginning to roll down her cheek as she mulls how the rest of her day will be. There's now no chance she'll be able to make it to her son's ballgame that afternoon and dreads the inevitable argument with her husband when she calls him in between patients to break the news. This is the second game she's missed in a row. If nothing changes, she might miss the rest of the season.

"I can't keep doing this," she thinks to herself, feeling her blood pressure climbing. Her stress and anxiety are getting to her.

She graduated from dental school with so much hope and excitement, but in the ten years since, something changed. She no longer feels excited about her work. On too many days, it feels like a grind. She enjoys helping patients, but there's so much more to her job than that. She has a solo practice and feels like she has to do everything herself. Her patient care is only a small part of her work week, and she feels crushed by the paperwork, budgeting, and other operational activities required of her. When she gets backed up with appointments, which seems to happen more and more often, nothing seems to go right.

In addition to her back pain, her doctor just put her on blood-pressure medication. Her marriage is under strain, as she and her husband are always fighting about her work and how it takes over their lives. She feels helpless and hopeless.

When she wraps up with the patient, she sticks her head into where Marie, her receptionist, sits. "Give me two minutes," she states, rushing to the restroom to splash water onto her face to try to calm her nerves before the next patient. After taking a few deep breaths, she stares into the mirror, takes another slow, deep breath, and unconvincingly attempts to reassure herself, "I can do this."

As she walks out to greet her next patient, she wonders whether she really can.

Dr. Scott's story is the reality for far too many dentists. Dentistry is a high-stress, high-risk profession where anxiety among patients and their dentists runs high. In fact, research tells us that the incidence of high blood pressure and coronary disease is twenty-five percent higher among dentists than the general population, and the effects of their work are causing havoc in their lives—their marriages are rocky, their health is in disarray, and their happiness is low.

As a practicing dentist, I know how stressful our work can be. We're taught the ideal of perfection in dental school and come out doing our best to attain it. Some might even have every intention to do excellent dentistry, but the dentistry is often rendered imperfect due to time and patient inattention or neglect.

Many of us got into this profession because we wanted to help people, but the reality of our work is we spend a lot of time doing much more than that. Those of us in small or solo practices often do *all* the work ourselves, taking care of patients, handling bills, budgets, marketing (when we can), inventory management, and a host of other activities we didn't anticipate as enthusiastic dental students. To make more money to try to keep up with rising overhead costs and repay student loans and practice debt, we take on as many patients as we can, often working through lunch, into the evening, and even on weekends. That only exacerbates our stress.

We hope things will improve someday, believing we're *paying our dues* and it will take time to build our practice revenues. But then we see dentists who have been practicing for more than twenty years, and it seems like too many of them are still working as hard as we are and fear there will be no end to the constant stress and strain.

This is a recipe for burnout. And it's the reason we see dentists who lose hope and hate their work. It's also the reason some dentists give up on the profession altogether and go off and do something else.

Is that the answer to this high-stress, high-risk work—that we need to either hate our lives or quit our profession?

I don't believe so.

There *is* another answer!

I wrote this book to help you find your answer so you don't waste the best years of your life stressed, depressed, and hopeless. The steps in this book can help you transform the way you work, how you live, and the return on your investment of the time, effort, and money you've put into your studies and business.

This book will help you get your patients to feel the *WOW* of your practice by teaching you how to deliver a *Delivering WOW* experience to everyone in your practice! The Delivering WOW experience uses innovative approaches and strategies to give your patients a WOW experience, generate more revenue, and create more free time for yourself, so you are no longer crushed under the weight and demand of patient appointments and administrative duties. With the added revenue you bring in by implementing the Delivering WOW experience into your practice, you can even build a practice that can run without your day-to-day, constant involvement. By implementing or outsourcing some of the simple but sophisticated tactics such as building dental-marketing funnels to turn strangers into patients while you sleep, you'll be able to get more control of your practice while shifting much of your marketing and onboarding time to serving new patients or taking a much-needed vacation! You'll have everything you need to *finally* build the practice you dreamed of when you were a young, hopeful dental student.

You'll have everything you need to go from burnout to balance.

To start, you need to shift the way you see your patients. No longer are they just patients. You must also see them as customers. This shift is important, because when we think of those we serve as patients, we can get a bit complacent and sometimes feel as if they *must* come to us because they need our help. Sometimes we can feel like we're the only one who can help them. If a patient has a toothache, he *must* go to a dentist. He can't go to a dermatologist or an internist. He *has* to come to us.

The problem with only seeing them as patients is it implies a sense of entitlement to their business, like customer service is unnecessary. That doesn't serve us well, and it doesn't serve our patients well. When you shift your mindset to viewing your patients as customers, you shift from thinking of them as people who must come to you to thinking of them as people who *choose to* come to you.

Thinking of your patients as customers also encourages you to communicate with them better to find out how to serve them better, keep them coming back, and turn them into raving fans who refer people to you. It helps you focus on what they want when they come to you and tells you how to communicate with them more effectively. No patient comes to you to buy a crown. They come to you to buy the peace of mind that their teeth won't break on their next vacation. They don't want scaling and root planing; they want peace of mind that their teeth won't get long or loose. This simple shift helps you look for ways you can Deliver WOW experiences to them, to delight them, so they come back and refer others to you. *Treat* them as patients by giving them the dental care they need, but always *see* them as customers whose business you must earn.

You do this by Delivering WOW to everyone who walks in your office. Delivering WOW is an approach I first implemented in my practice, Jamaica Cosmetic Dental Services, before sharing it with other dentists and small-business owners so they could implement the concept in their offices. Delivering WOW focuses on six essential areas of business, including your practice's Vision, Culture, Core Values, Team, Systems, and Brand. When you implement the Delivering WOW experience in these key areas, you'll see a remarkable difference in the quality of your practice.

CHAPTER 2

Action Was My Middle Name!

My journey as a dentist began when I graduated from the University of Alabama School of Dentistry in 1999. When I got out of dental school, I was ready to take on the world. I was ready to put into practice all that I had learned. I was ready to give back and help others. I was ready to make a difference! I decided to remain in Birmingham and had the fortunate opportunity to work in several types of practices. One was a very fast-paced, low-fee practice. It was very focused on money. I would often hear the office manager say, "We need to make $10,000 today." I was very uncomfortable in that environment. I knew that money was important, but the core could not be the money. It had to be the people. Relationships. That practice was about high volume and money goals. Needless to say, I left that practice after only six months.

From there, I went to work for a dentist who was really big into cosmetic dentistry and customer service. We did things like bake cookies so that the office would smell like home. We read books like *Raving Fans* by Ken Blanchard and went to seminars with Dr. Tom Orent. With that opportunity, my eyes were opened, and the foundation was laid. After about a year at that practice, I opened my own office and decided I would focus on providing both excellent care and great service.

I enjoyed beautifying people's smiles and changing their lives. I set up the waiting area like a living room and served coffee, tea, and baked cookies. From the very beginning, I thought about ways to create uniqueness and at the same time be profitable.

One of the ways I found to grow my practice was to look for underserved populations I could serve. That way, I could be a larger fish in a smaller pond. I did a little research and discovered there weren't many dentists who were providers for kids with Medicaid in Birmingham. That was a great opportunity for me because it allowed me to grow my practice while serving people whom many other dentists were not willing to serve. That was exactly the impact I was looking to make with my practice, so I dedicated one full day each week to treating these incredible kids with the same care and attention we gave all of our VIP patients.

Another way I found to grow my practice in a way that also gave back to an underserved market was to set up a strategic alliance with a local pediatric dentist to refer all of their teenage patients to us, many of whom were foster kids who were brought in by their social workers. It felt really great to give these kids a great experience and give them the VIP treatment.

We were one of the few dental offices where teenagers with Medicaid could get their wisdom teeth removed. My husband, an oral surgery resident at the time, would come in on Saturdays to treat them. We received so much love from these children, even more than the love and respect with which we treated them. Those children changed all of our lives, and we're so grateful we had the opportunity to serve them. And as valuable and appreciated as the love we received from those children was, our pediatric Medicaid practice because a huge profit center.

A third underserved population we discovered that allowed us to create a profitable strategic uniqueness to our practice was a large Spanish-speaking immigrant population. One of my hygienists, Mayra, was a dentist who had trained in Mexico but was unable to practice dentistry in Alabama because she did not have a U.S. dental degree. When she joined my practice, I sent her to receive her dental hygiene training and license. One day, Mayra came to me with the brilliant idea that we place an ad in the local Spanish newspaper. She said there were many Spanish-speaking members of the community, but no dental office that focused on treating them. She shared that it could be very frustrating for them to be unable to communicate with their doctor, and she wanted to help them. We decided we would be the office that welcomed them, and we did. Eventually, everyone in the office spoke Spanish. I even took classes and learned to speak Spanish to better communicate with those patients. Like the other underserved populations, we saw a need, filled it, and built another patient population that was grateful to find an office that cared about them, and in this case, where the team could communicate effectively with them. They, in turn, became "raving fans," and spread the word about our practice.

As I had done with the patients who had Medicaid, I was willing to serve an underserved market. I served people who had been overlooked by other providers. As a result of doing something different, we became very profitable from very early on.

In 2005, my husband and I decided to move to Jamaica. My husband, an oral and maxillofacial surgeon, grew up in Jamaica. With only one or two oral surgeons on the island, he knew that Jamaica would be where he could make the greatest impact, so we decided we would move there to potentially make it our permanent home. I knew I could build a profitable practice in Jamaica just like I had stateside, so I committed to going and learning the dental market there while we decided if we would live there permanently. If we did, I committed to opening a practice the same way I operated in Alabama. I knew that with a quick one-hour flight, I would be able to get back stateside for continuing education and would have easy access to the same dental suppliers and labs I used when my practice was in Birmingham, so I knew I could utilize the relationships I had built in Alabama and the systems I put in place in another setting to make a meaningful impact while building a profitable practice.

I started working in Jamaica as an independent contractor in a well-established practice to learn the business culture of Jamaica. After five years, my husband and I realized Jamaica would be our permanent home, so I decided to start a new practice, Jamaica Cosmetic Dental Services.

I started this practice in an 800-square-foot space with only three operatories. For two years, we built a great practice in our small office, while I dreamed and planned our next move. As in Alabama, we achieved a traditional slow and steady growth path for a dental office, creatively looking for underserved markets, being more efficient and effective with traditional dental marketing, and delivering top-quality dental care and experiences.

After two years, I had an "aha" moment. I had come to Jamaica to make an impact, yet I wasn't doing anything very impactful. Although we steadily grew, by taking a traditional approach, we achieved traditional results. I worked a lot and even struggled a bit managing cash flow. I knew there were certain areas I needed to put money to grow the business. Unfortunately, I always had to balance what needed to be purchased with having cash in the bank.

I realized if I wanted different results, I needed to take a different approach, so I decided to take action. I walked into the practice and announced to my team that we were moving.

They said, "Dr. Holmes, we just moved to this office."

My response was, "I know, but I have a *big* vision."

My vision was for our practice to be the top dental practice in the country while being known for Delivering WOW experiences to our patients. As driven and experienced as I was both in patient care and building a profitable practice, I knew it wasn't smart to try to do everything myself, especially with such a big vision, so I decided to get a business coach to help me.

Over the next year, I worked with my coach to design and implement a plan to achieve my vision to be the top dental practice in Jamaica and known for Delivering WOW experiences to our patients. Within one year, we doubled our revenue and tripled our capacity to a 2,500-square foot space, which I committed to building out without borrowing money. Perhaps I could have grown faster had I borrowed, but that's not the path I wanted to take. I accepted that things would be tight. I committed to reinvesting profits into the business to buy equipment. I made personal sacrifices to hold off on spending and put that money into the company.

Before I decided to get a coach, I was a typical dentist, thinking if I provided high-quality dentistry and gave good service, my database of patients would grow. Although I saw *some* growth, I knew there was more I could do in that area.

At the beginning of my coaching relationship, my coach and I dissected my business, carefully looking at how I was running each element of it to determine whether each of those elements would bring me closer to achieving my big vision. When I did that, I realized the traditional, slow-growth approach many dentists were taking just wasn't going to work for me if I wanted to achieve my vision, at least not any time soon. I wanted to build a great business to enjoy *then*, not wait a dozen more years.

We also worked on identifying multiple growth strategies in order to multiply my business rather than sticking to just one strategy, even if that one strategy was effective. We studied and experimented with many different growth strategies to find the ones that achieved the best results for the time and money required. When we found the right mix, everything changed. We started turning hundreds of dollars into thousands of dollars over and over again. We started receiving regular and predictable patient growth and having patients rave about us to their friends and family. The manner in which we studied and implemented multiple growth strategies within the context of our big vision eventually led to what we now call building a Delivering WOW! practice, which is the exact process I'm describing in this book.

When we committed to build a Delivering WOW practice, focusing on building our culture, systems, and brand, our growth skyrocketed. The month before I wrote the first edition, we welcomed more than 250 new patients. That's a number a lot of practices would dream of having over several months or even a year, and we got that number in just one month.

We were also able to leverage creative marketing tactics to regularly turn a marketing budget of $500 into returns of up to $8,000. That's a 1,500 percent return on our investment! Moreover, by implementing multiple growth strategies, we discovered one that increased revenue by $20,000 a month. We would never have used that new strategy if we had stuck with using just one strategy, even if that one strategy had performed well. These are just three of many examples of what can happen when you begin to Deliver WOW in your practice.

I'll share the exact steps of how I produced those numbers later in this book, along with additional tactics that my dental coaching clients, Inner Circle Mastermind members, and Delivering WOW Platinum Coaching Program members have utilized to achieve explosive practice growth. Before I do so, it's important to share a little more about my experience as you start to think of your own practice because, although increasing profit is important, profit is only one benefit of building a Delivering WOW practice. In fact, as great as the profits I've earned have been, I've received infinitely more personal satisfaction than just money.

Specifically, building a Delivering WOW practice allows you to achieve time freedom and an ability to give back to your community and worthy causes in a way that can't always be measured by bank-account balances. For example, the ability to attend school events or take an extra vacation with your family and the ability to give away dental services to needy members of my community because I don't have to worry about bills being paid are all incredibly rewarding benefits I mainly attribute to Delivering WOW. Before I implemented the strategies in this book, I was like many of the dentists I know: working way too many hours, feeling the pressure of increasing overhead costs, frustrated about missing time with my family, and feeling like I didn't have the ability to give much back to my community because I needed to perform paid work. However, I was not okay with that. I knew there must be a better way, a way to make a great living while living a great life.

From very early on, I wanted to be a doctor, but I also wanted to live a great life and contribute to my community. While in college, I had an excellent opportunity to attend a summer program at the dental school at the University of Alabama. As part of that program, I was able to spend the summer working in the pediatric dental clinic. I met an amazing resident, Dr. Sanchez, who shared with me her passion for treating kids and for dentistry. She also shared that dentistry was a great profession, as it offered a lot of flexibility to have a balanced life. She also talked a lot about the ability to make a difference and help the community.

The idea of helping others had always been important to me. I did lots of community service in high school, and while in dental school, I went to Central America to do mission work. My chosen profession seemed a perfect fit to continue helping others.

However, like many dentists, once I was running my practice, I found that my income wasn't what I wanted, and I didn't always feel like I had the time to help others in the way I dreamed. Yes, I created beautiful smiles and helped patients reduce or eliminate their fear. But I focused too much time working *in* and not *on* my business. I was too busy being busy to slow down and build my business into something that gave me more time *and* money.

Delivering WOW has helped me do just that. Since developing and implementing Delivering WOW into my office, I built a dedicated and fantastic team, and together we Deliver WOW to patients day in and day out. The practice has grown steadily and significantly since adopting this new approach. We even had to hire additional hygienists and dentists to keep up with demand while maintaining the same level of VIP service we promise to all of our patients. That significantly increased our revenue and profits but resulted in my having much more free time than I did before—time to spend with my family, connect with friends, or invest in other activities of my choosing. My practice can run well whether I am in the office or away, all because of the principles and techniques in this book!

So, what exactly is Delivering WOW? Well, that's what the next chapter answers . . .

DELIVERING WOW ACTION ACTIVITY:

Take an honest look at your life today. Are you happy? How has your practice affected your personal life? Write just what kind of impact your practice has on your life and what you would like to change.

CHAPTER 3

What is Delivering WOW?

Are you tired of doing the same old things and getting the same results? Do you want to have more freedom? Do you wish to know the secret to success? Well, it all starts with Delivering WOW.

Delivering WOW means that your ultimate vision is to create a practice that can run without you. This doesn't mean that you will stop practicing dentistry, although some who achieve this level of success choose to do so. It means that your practice is so efficient that if you were to decide to take a vacation for six months, your team and systems could run your practice. It means that you go to work because you *want* to, and not because you *have* to. It means that your patients have peace of mind because the dentistry that you provide is meticulous, beautiful, and long-lasting. It means that you have a unique culture known for providing extraordinary experiences even for the most fearful patients and that your patients grow your business for you. Does this seem like a dream? Well, listen up, because it can be your reality.

Delivering WOW is a customer-focused, results-oriented approach that service businesses such as dental practices can use to provide a consistently high level of service and excellence to those they serve without sacrificing profitability or lifestyle. Delivering WOW focuses on building relationships and taking action in six core areas and can revolutionize how you run your business.

To implement Delivering WOW into your practice, it's critical that you take the time to master each step before moving onto the next, as they build upon each other. For example, no great business owner has built a remarkable brand without first having a vision for their company. Additionally, you must have top-quality operations and team members before utilizing the marketing techniques I teach in order to be able to serve your new patients with the same great service you do with your existing patients. If not, you could disappoint new and existing patients.

By implementing Delivering WOW into your practice the way I teach you here, you can quickly transform a struggling, cash-strapped practice into a dynamic practice that experiences massive growth and turn an ordinary practice into a leading dental office in your community. The reason this approach works is because it focuses on specific areas that affect the business's relationship with its customers: Vision, Culture, Core Values, Team, Systems, and Brand. With each of those in place, you'll be in a great position to market your practice with confidence that you can serve new patients well.

I'll give you specific details for each step of the Delivering WOW experience later, but let me tell you why each area is so important first, so you can understand the importance of working on each area in order to provide WOW experiences for your patients and achieve more for your life.

Vision is the first step of the Delivering WOW experience and, perhaps, the most important. Your vision is your *big* dream for your practice. Your vision as a dentist will affect your entire practice as well as your future growth. Your vision will also influence the speed at which you will achieve your personal dreams. If you do not have a vision, then anything can happen, because there is no detailed roadmap of how you will achieve your goals. Your vision is the big idea you have for your business, and ultimately, your life.

Culture is the second step of the Delivering WOW experience and important because it's the story you want to tell people about your practice. It's what you want to be known for. Every practice has a culture, whether you create it or it evolves. Being focused on your company culture helps ensure that you're developing an environment to bring forth your vision.

The third step in the Delivering WOW experience is creating your core values. Your core values are the rules of your company. They declare what your practice stands for, and they are used when making all of the decisions for your practice. Core values are also important because they help you live out your culture, and they are critical to achieving your vision. For example, if one of your core values is "pursue growth and learning," and a team member continuously refuses to attend continuing-education courses, they would be operating outside your core values and would not be a good fit for your practice.

Once you've clearly defined your vision, culture, and core values, your next step is to *align your team* to your vision, culture, and core values. Some of you already have a great team to help you develop the core values for your practice. Others may realize that some shifts may have to be made to your current team in order to achieve your vision and build your culture in accordance with your core values. The key point is all members of your team must be aligned with the practice's vision for it to be achieved. It can't be *your* vision alone; it has to be the vision of everyone in your practice, even if you developed the vision to begin with. Your team needs to share that vision. It's also vital for your team to have personal visions for themselves and know they can achieve their dreams by working in your practice.

Once you know where you're headed and have the right team, the next step is to look at your systems. Systems are essential for scaling up your operations, providing consistent services, increasing profits, reducing costs, and serving more patients. If you're stuck and feel as if you have to do every single thing in your practice, it's because you don't have the proper systems in place. If you're providing inconsistent experiences to patients, this is also a weakness that's showing up because of lack of adequate systems. If you want consistency in your practice, or if you wish to create a practice that can run without you, you *must* have written systems in place.

The next step of the Delivering WOW experience is to develop a fascinating brand. When the first five steps work together, the result is your brand. Most people mistake the term *brand* to refer to a logo or catch phrase. It's not. Your brand is what people say about you when you're not around.

Your logo might remind them of your brand, but your brand is not your logo. Your brand is how people feel when they describe your company. It's what attracts your ideal patients. Creating a fascinating brand will separate you from the next dental practice in the mind of your patients. When you've developed a fascinating brand by Delivering WOW, internal and external marketing are great ways to share your brand and let the world know all of the fascinating things that you are doing. This newly updated and expanded edition of Delivering WOW has some of the best and most efficient marketing techniques to do just that.

By the way, can you guess what the ultimate goal of the Delivering WOW experience is? Yes, it's achieving your vision. Everything points to achieving your vision and everything is filtered through that goal.

Delivering WOW is about helping you to build a fascinating brand. It's about getting more done in less time. It's about positioning your business as something unique within your community. Take our practice, for example. Our vision is to be the leading dental practice in Jamaica known for Delivering WOW.

Our work in the area of WOW experiences has positioned us in the community as a dental office that is very different. The same can be for your practice, no matter where you are located. What WOW means for your practice may be different than what WOW means for mine. But the common thread is that WOW will be about exceptional service and superior care. From the moment a patient enters our office, our goal is to WOW them. The patient is welcomed with a smile, offered a beverage such as hot chocolate, gourmet tea, or Café Blue coffee— among Jamaica's finest coffee—and invited to enjoy a freshly baked plantain tart.

We also know some patients experience anxiety when they visit a dentist, so we provide iPads to take away the sound as well as hand-and-arm massages to take away tension and relax their minds. We offer new toothbrushes in the restroom so patients can brush, and we offer scented lotions and perfumes so they can feel at home.

These amenities make up the WOW experience customers *see*, but there's so much more to Delivering WOW in our office. Medical offices are notorious for being off schedule. It's not uncommon for patients to wait an exceptionally long time before being seen. We realize this and want our patients to know we value their time just as much as they do, so we offer an on-time guarantee. If a patient is not seated within fifteen minutes of his or her appointment time, their next exam is free.

These are just some of the offerings we have put in place to set our practice apart and to WOW our customers. And it works! We regularly get five-star ratings and feedback from customers commenting on the special way in which they were treated. This translates to more word-of-mouth advertising and more customers.

That's what WOWing customers looks like in our office. In your office, it might be something different. But whatever it is, it needs to be something unique that goes beyond what others are doing. That's the true nature of Delivering WOW. It's about truly being a cut above. It's about being unique. It's about being different.

You may be wondering how it is possible to add so many amenities or do something like providing an on-time guarantee in a dental practice. Well, that's what the next several chapters will explain. The next chapters will describe in detail the six core areas, so you see how each fit into the overall WOW experience and helps you to do what you need to do to stand out.

Are you ready? Let's get to it!

DELIVERING WOW ACTION ACTIVITY:

Evaluate your readiness for making fundamental changes in your practice. Are you willing to change the way you operate? Are you ready to do the hard work of putting in place certain actions, systems, and processes to overhaul your practice? Why or why not?

CHAPTER 4

Vision

What is your vision? What is that one big goal that you want to achieve for your life? Have you clearly defined it? Is it written? As dentists, many of us just go to work day in and day out, and before we realize it, years have passed, but we are in the same place. We still haven't taken that European vacation, we still haven't paid off our credit cards, and we still are not spending enough time with those who matter most. So, what happened? Well, we didn't plan—I mean really plan—for success. It was more like "At some point, I will . . ." versus setting goals with a roadmap of how we would get there. The reason I discuss personal vision first is because for most of us, our practice will provide the income for us to achieve our personal dreams.

I went through life knowing I wanted to be successful. But that was it. I didn't define exactly what success was. I wasn't specific about what success would look like. I wasn't taking steps to reach specific goals. I thought if I was serving my community and making my patients happy, then I'd have a successful practice. However, once I set a clearly defined vision with an extremely specific goal, I was able to achieve so much more, and in less time. I now even have a physical vision board that shows the vision I want for my life in picture form. My vision board has photos of places that I'd like to visit and experiences I'd like to have with my family.

My vision was very specific for my practice, and it's what I shared with you in an earlier chapter: to be the leading dental practice in Jamaica known for Delivering WOW. Once I committed to implementing what became the process you're learning in order to achieve my personal and practice visions, all I had to do was determine how I'd get there.

Having both personal and practice visions is important, because sometimes dentists develop a practice vision that doesn't take their personal goals into account. If you do that, you might achieve your big practice vision and realize your personal life is suffering. Thus, once you create your personal vision, it's time to create one for your business.

As you evolve as a practice leader, you must learn to think more strategically and clearly. If your vision is to be successful, then you have to define success to know what to do next. What do you want to achieve in one year, in five, or perhaps when you retire? Not only write what you want but paint a clear picture of your vision in your mind and see yourself achieving it. Visualize your success. If you can dream it, you can achieve it!

So how can you go from a vague idea of being successful, to living out your vision?

1. **Clearly define your vision.** It isn't enough to simply say that you want to be successful. You must be specific. Visualizing what you intend to achieve will help you know what you are working toward, as well as will help you determine priorities. Be sure to define a vision for your personal life, too.

2. **Write out your vision.** When you are setting your vision, it's important to write it down. Writing your vision puts it in a tangible form you can see and feel. That's exactly what happened to me.

3. **See it in picture form.** Creating a vision board will allow you to activate yourself in a way that merely seeing the vision written in words alone cannot. The exercise of creating a vision board will help you engage your senses and focus your mind on the task in front of you.

4. **Create your plan.** What do you need to do to ensure that you achieve your goal? For us to become the leading dental practice in Jamaica, we had to build a new office. We had to determine what would be unique about the practice to make us stand out. We had to create specific systems and practices that would encourage a consistent delivery of a WOW experience.

5. **Act on the plan.** Be very specific about the goals that you'd like to achieve and who will help you achieve them, and then set a deadline by when they must be accomplished. Make sure to write which action items must be checked off daily, weekly, or monthly until your goal is achieved. Each of these steps is significant in going from merely wishing and wanting something, to creating a clear vision, and then to actually making it happen.

A vision without action is just passing time. Your business has not finished its growth and development until your vision becomes a reality. From there, your vision will grow, and you can then set new goals for your business. Not only do you need to create a personal vision and a vision for your practice, but you also need to inspire your team to create personal visions for themselves. They need to see how being a part of the practice's vision can help them achieve their personal goals.

Get to Your "Why."

Do you want more time, money, or freedom? Exploring your why will help define your priorities, aspirations, and in turn, your vision. When it comes to the vision you have for your life and your practice, take the time to clearly define what you want to achieve. If you're having trouble determining your vision, start with your "why." Why is reaching this goal important to you? What will achieving this goal provide for you?

Once you know what you are working for, then you naturally become very excited about seeing it come to life. My big why to achieving my personal vision is that I want the freedom to travel the world with my family; I want to leave a legacy for my future generations. When I celebrate my 80th birthday, I want people to share stories of how I impacted their lives. Once I got to my why, it was easy to create my vision. Next, I had to take action steps to achieve it.

Unfortunately, many people do not look ahead. They are going to work day after day earning an income, and that's it. That's all they see for themselves. There is no vision there. However, you don't have to be one of those people. Once you have a clear picture of why you are working, your life begins to have more purpose. Once you have a vision of what you want, you find a way, whether it's through reading more books, having a coach help you to fast-track your success, getting more training, or joining a mastermind.

Life is About Balance!

Having a balanced life is about being fulfilled, not just through your business, but being fulfilled in your personal life, too, so you live without regret. For me, it means spending time with my family and friends, exercising, and otherwise being healthy.

Some people put way too much time into their business and have no time left for the other areas of their lives. They don't put time or effort into growing their marriages, so their marriages suffer. They neglect their health, so they end up with illnesses or debilitating conditions as result of this neglect. They aren't giving their children time, so there are regrets once their kids are all grown up and they realize that they never took the time to have great conversations or that they missed critical events.

Indeed, creating a vision for your life helps you to assess just where you are and what you need to change. Your business isn't your whole life. It's just one part of your life. It's a vehicle to help you achieve your personal dreams. Your business is what gives you the freedom to spend more time on what matters most, not to take you away from those things.

More Strategies for Success: The Success Wheel

When looking at life, there are so many daily and weekly tasks that you can use to fill your time. I like to see life as a pie, with many different slices that make it complete. Every slice is vital to capturing the full essence of the pie—your life.

Some of the slices of the pie of life are time at work, time with a spouse, time with kids, time with friends, time to exercise, personal development, spiritual practice, meditation, and contributing to the community. You can download a copy of the success wheel on the resources page at DeliveringWOW.com/WOWResources.

Do you find that your life is unbalanced? Are there areas where you know you need to spend more time? Even if you find that you are happy overall, there may still be one or two areas you want to work on.

If your child were chosen to be the lead in a school play or chosen for an elite sports group, you would probably find a way to get them to the activity. However, we as adults often say we're too busy to do things that bring us happiness or better health. The thing is, there's never enough time to do *everything*, but there's *always* time to do what matters most.

One tool you can use to ensure that you accomplish what matters most is to create a default diary. A default diary is a plan where you schedule important tasks at set times, so they get done. The idea is we're often so busy doing low-priority or urgent tasks that we never get around to doing what's necessary and beneficial to our long-term growth. So, the default diary sets a predetermined time for doing these important activities.

For me, I found that I was working so much I didn't spend time with friends. So, in my default diary, I set aside time every Wednesday night to spend time with friends, whether that was dinner or some other activity. I also set aside from 5–7p.m. every weekday to focus on spending time with my kids.

Visit the resources page for a template to create your default diary. With this default diary, you can schedule patient-treatment time, time to work *on* your business, and all of the other important things, such as exercise, date night, and time with your family. Don't let anything encroach on these nonnegotiables, as they are what you have defined as what matters most. Your systems can make your business successful, but these will be the things that make you happy and healthy.

Have your team create their personal diaries, too, mapping out what they will accomplish during the workday as well as in their personal lives.

When you use a default diary to help implement your vision, you find that there *is* time to do all of the most important things you want to do. A lot of people say, "I don't have time," but it's because they are spending time on things that don't matter.

This one tip—using a default diary—can transform the way you work and live, so if you set a vision but feel that you have no way of achieving it because you feel you don't have the time, then consider this tip. A default diary can not only help you get to your vision, it can also help you avoid many of the traps others in our profession experience—burnout, poor relationships, and poor health.

Break Your Vision Down into Stages

In my practice, once we set our big goal to be the leading practice known for Delivering WOW, we knew that the next step was to take action. We put in place a passionate team. We overhauled our entire office, picking apart and implementing new procedures, training our team on various aspects of the WOW experience, and more.

It's important to break down your vision into stages. If you simply approach your vision as that big, final attainment, it can be difficult to know how to get there. But if you break it down into stages, let's say you break it down into years, then it can be a lot easier to manage, and it can be a lot more likely that you will realize that vision.

For instance, in my case, I plan my next year the December before. From there, I break my goals down by quarters, then by months, and then by weeks. This helps me know what to do and what to focus on at any given time. I look at fifteen things I want to happen that quarter and then plan it. Of course, this doesn't mean I must personally do each of these things. My team does many of these tasks. We will discuss team a bit later in this book, but your team can be your number-one asset.

If you're setting a vision and want to be in a particular place in five years, for example, determine where you need to be in three years, and then where you need to be in one year, in order for you to be where you want to be five years from now. From there, break your next year down even more. Be sure to set a vision for your personal life as well as your business, as the two are intertwined.

Finally, don't be discouraged if a life event throws you off the plan a little. Life happens. Sometimes you plan for a particular event or activity to happen in one month, but it can't happen that month because of the life event. That's okay. Don't let your plans stall because not everything falls into place just the way you had it on the schedule. Just be flexible and shift that activity to the next time it can happen. Push forward the best you can. Something will go wrong. Don't give up.

When you plan in this way, you can look back on the weeks, months, quarters, and years and realize just how much you've accomplished. This is important, because sometimes we get so focused on a big goal we don't take time to appreciate all the smaller but still worthwhile accomplishments we make in our personal and professional lives. You can make those accomplishments because you took the time to break down big goals into small goals. Also, don't be surprised if you achieve more goals and in a shorter time than you planned if you follow this system.

Create Vision and Mission Statements

Once you have developed your vision for your business, it's helpful to create a vision statement and mission statement for your office. Your vision statement is a short statement that speaks to the aspirations of the company. Include the vision you have for the company as well as how it will affect the lives of your patients, the community, or others. Your vision statement should be aspirational, something bold that inspires others. It puts to words the big thing you're working toward. Write this out in one succinct, clear sentence.

Your mission statement is a statement about *why* you exist and helps you focus on your big idea. The mission statement takes its cue from your vision. The mission statement should be clear and specific. Think of your vision as the future state you hope to attain and the mission as the state you will be in at all times while doing the work to achieve your vision. In other words, it's your commitment as a business to operating in a certain way. If your vision is to be the best practice in your area, your mission might be to deliver the best patient care in a way that makes going to the dentist a relaxing experience for all of your patients. Your mission statement is personal to you and your practice and describes behavior or activities you can live by every day that will naturally lead to you achieving your vision. It's the work you're doing now that's consistent with your visions in order to achieve your vision.

Inspire Your Team's Vision

It's important to engage those in your vision who will play a significant role in helping you to accomplish it. In the case of a dental practice, this is primarily your team. Be sure to help your team see how your overall vision for the business will help them to accomplish their personal and professional goals. I often speak of vision at our office, and my team is just as excited about it as I am because it's become a shared vision. We all want to have the best dental practice in the country, and we all see how accomplishing that and Delivering WOW will improve each of our lives. My team understands that as our business becomes more profitable, they can earn more money because I share the increasing profits with them, which can enable them to do things in their lives to achieve their personal dreams. When you think big and you write down what you want and focus on what matters most, you achieve your goals.

Once you start to look at your vision, you begin to dream. Your thinking will expand, and you'll be able to achieve things you never thought possible. Your vision will evolve as you grow, too. Mine did. This is the power of vision.

DELIVERING WOW ACTION ACTIVITY:

Take the time to write your vision for your personal life. Make a list of all of the activities you do that make you happy. Next, make a list of all of the activities you do every day. Now compare the two lists. Do you need to make a shift?

From there, focus on and write a big vision for your practice.

Talk to your team about your vision for the practice, establishing a vision for their personal and professional lives and how the practice can help them achieve their personal dreams.

Have your team create vision boards by cutting and pasting pictures of places they'd like to go, experiences they'd like to have, and things they'd like to purchase. Do the same for your vision. Take a group photo of everyone holding their vision boards, and post it to your social media pages, such as Facebook, Instagram, Twitter, and Google Plus.

Display your vision board in your office and share it during new-patient office tours.

On a scale of one to ten, with ten being the happiest, write how happy you are in each area of your life. Next to your current number, write where you want to be in one year. This exercise will show you where you need to focus over the next twelve months.

CHAPTER 5

Culture

We grew up with a myth! This myth is that to be successful, we must be better than everyone else. We must try harder and work longer. We must be better in school, be better than our teammates, and be better than other applicants. We have been conditioned to copy what others are doing, and then try to do that same thing better.

The reality is being *unique* is better than being better. Being unique will get you more than being the best will.

While businesses have put a lot of focus on being "better," customers are focusing on something entirely different. They're focusing on getting the best deal. They're looking at all of the options that are the same and choosing the cheapest option.

When you can successfully differentiate yourself, however, you become the go-to person or company for one particular reason. That's when you can charge higher fees. That's when you can dominate your market. That's when you realize being different is better than being "better."

One of the first steps to standing out and being different is by creating the story you want to tell about your practice: Your culture.

In building a dynamic dental practice, culture has to be top of mind when you're planning the transformation of your business. Once you create your culture, you will attract team members and patients who are aligned with or can identify with that culture, because they'll feel an emotional connection with your business.

To build a fascinating brand, start with your culture. Leading brands clearly point out their differences. These differences can be small, but they must be clearly defined. The fact is, people can replicate your services, your systems can be beaten, and people can outdo your strengths, but nobody can copy who you are.

Decide what will be unique about your practice. Will it be a phenomenal patient experience, an on-time guarantee, or additional services other offices in your community aren't providing? Think about the experience you have when you go to Starbucks. It's more than just the coffee that draws people in. People have an emotional connection. It's the aroma; it's how the baristas make you feel.

Culture can mean different things to different dental practices. For us, it's about VIP amenities and treating every patient like family. It's about the way we make patients feel by providing iPads and Bluetooth headphones to take away the sound, or complimentary arm-and-hand massages to relax patients before their dental visit. We've put a lot of thought into our culture and how we can be unique. We even have a coffee table culture book in our reception area for patients to see photos of us having fun behind the scenes or out building stronger communities.

When building our culture, it was important for us to find out what our patients wanted—what mattered most—so we could focus on it. So, we asked them! We asked patients while in our office, polled our Facebook fans, and sent out surveys to patients the day after their appointments asking how we could serve them better. We found out there were different priorities for different patients, but the answers were consistent. Our patients wanted three things:

1. To be seen on time. Some of our patients are busy. They don't have a lot of time. What mattered most for them was being seen on time or being given a phone call if we knew we would be running behind schedule.
2. To have quality and consistency of their dental services. They wanted their dental work to be beautiful, look natural, and be long-lasting. They wanted "peace of mind."
3. To have a great experience. Many patients have had bad experiences and are extremely fearful when going to the dentist. What mattered most to them was finding a dental home that could take care of their dental concerns with little to no pain.

After finding out what mattered most to our patients, we built our culture around that. We stocked our coffee and tea bar with gourmet Blue Mountain coffee, specialty teas, hot chocolate, and freshly baked plantain tarts. We stocked our bathrooms with toothbrushes, scented lotions, and perfumes. We finish every patient visit by treating our patients with a relaxing warm peppermint-scented towel.

We also implemented an on-time guarantee. If patients aren't seen within fifteen minutes of their appointment time, their next exam is free. To make this happen, we had to have the right team in place to carry patients to the treatment area on time and to start with the office tour, Xrays, patient-education videos, and the hand massages. We also call patients when we know we are running behind to adjust the time they should arrive. The patients appreciate this courtesy, because it shows them we value their time.

One of the other essential elements of our culture is our team. We invest in our team, and it shows. We constantly praise our team, be it face-to-face, in front of patients, or on social media. My team recently attended a dental conference, and they felt like celebrities because teams from other offices kept coming up to them and calling them by name after recognizing them from our social media channels!

One of my team members shared a story that in the office where she used to work, employees always had to look like they were busy, even if there was "nothing to do." And the lunch hour was strictly adhered to; employees had to be sure to eat and get back to work within that time. That's not our culture. If you're thirsty, and there is no patient who needs your attention, it's okay to get a cup of tea. Our practice is not a place where team members have to pretend to be busy or suffer hunger pangs simply because of the clock on the wall. Our team takes care of our patients, and we take care of our team. If that sometimes requires us to work through lunch or stay late to get the job done, nobody complains, because we all share the same vision and build a culture that values them. That's the culture we have.

We used to have to search hard for people to hire, but we now have individuals who work for other dentists calling us because they know about our culture. They call to ask, "What do I have to do to be a part of your team?"

We're also known for being charitable. We have given away smile makeovers and built a playground and computer lab for a school. We donate proceeds from new-patient exams to a different charity every month. In giving, we receive. Building communities is part of our story.

What Story Are You Telling?
What Culture Will You Create?

Culture isn't just about what your customers see. While culture ultimately *shows up* in what your customers see, it starts behind the scenes. Culture begins with what goes on in your practice from how you treat your employees to how they treat each other and how your office functions. If your team is unhappy or there is a lot of backbiting or drama, that will spill over into the experience your customers have. You can't have a negative internal company culture and present a positive customer experience. It just doesn't happen.

Every company has a culture. Sometimes it's designed. Other times it evolves on its own. We've all been to a business where employees were rude or it looked like they felt they were doing us a favor by serving us. Other times, we might go to a business and observe that the facility isn't clean, the service is subpar, or the quality of the product or service was nothing special. Maybe it was a restaurant. Maybe it was a clothing store. Maybe it was a dental office. Each of those businesses has a culture that evolved on its own, and it's not a positive culture. Maybe the business owner is absent or hasn't taken the time to think about the story they want their business to tell. As a result, things "just happen."

You don't want things just to happen in your practice, because what happens is out of your control, and you'll end up with a subpar, default culture. A default culture will never contribute to a WOW experience for your customers.

Building a great culture starts at the top. It begins with you as the leader. Decide what you want to be known for and enlist your team to help you create and share your story.

So how do you do that? Well, in addition to making sure you are treating employees with respect, it's also important to make sure you provide the tools they need to succeed in your office. I will discuss this more in the team chapter, but does everyone know his or her job description? Does everyone have the right resources to do the tasks you have assigned? Do employees feel as if their opinions matter and that they are heard when they have something to say? All of this contributes to the environment and culture you create.

As your business grows, the importance of culture grows. That's because the culture can be a significant factor in just how your company moves forward. Culture affects not only the types of customers you attract but also the kinds of employees you attract. If you want the best employees, then you'll need to make sure you are providing the best work environment. This isn't necessarily about putting in a lot of the amenities we see in some places like Silicon Valley and tech companies, like game rooms, catered meals, and the like. This is about creating an environment of open communication, functional operations, and an investment in the professional development of your employees.

At our office, we instituted weekly lunch-and-learns where we work on systems, discuss a book we're all reading, or do some other activity that helps the team learn together. That spirit of learning started with me, because as the leader of the practice, I had to first be a good example. I turned my car into a driving university where I listen to books on Audible or podcasts while commuting. I even listen while working out. The learning doesn't stop at the office, because now we have a culture of learning there as well. I even purchased Kindle e-readers for my team.

Instituting the lunch-and-learns, purchasing Kindles for the team, and setting aside time for team development is an investment I'm happy to make, because I know it'll pay off personally for my team as well as for the company.

The Importance of Culture in Achieving Your Vision

Once you have built a fascinating company culture that consistently exceeds patients' expectations and have the right team members who are in line with the company culture, your vision will be easy to achieve. Your patients will become "raving fans" and won't stop sharing stories about their experiences in your office. Your culture, once done right, builds your brand, which gets you one step closer to achieving your vision.

Delivering WOW in Action

Glenn Vo
Denton Smiles Dentistry
Denton, Texas
DentonSmilesDentistry.com

I started working with Dr. Anissa Holmes with the goals of creating a winning culture and becoming a better leader for my dental practice. Within one year, I completely changed the culture of my practice and increased production by $100,000. I did all of this while working *less* in my practice.

Even better, working with Anissa as a coach helped me make two life-changing discoveries about myself. First, I discovered I was passionate about helping other dentists navigate the financial minefield of practice ownership. Second, I discovered my ability to connect with others on multiple levels was a hidden talent I could use to pursue my passion for helping dentists.

With Anissa's guidance and direction, I started the Nifty Thrifty Dentists Facebook group and built it to more than 14,000 members. I also launched the Nifty Thrifty Dentists podcast, built a loyal audience, and have reached the top ranking in iTunes on multiple occasions. Finally, I have even begun speaking at industry conferences and events, such as Voices of Dentistry and the first ever Delivering WOW Summit in Jamaica.

Together, my Facebook group, podcast, and speaking engagements help thousands of dentists save money through camaraderie and group discounts.

A good coach helps you achieve your goals. A *great* coach does that *and* helps you unleash your potential.

I'm unleashing my potential by working with a great coach, Dr. Anissa Holmes.

DELIVERING WOW ACTION ACTIVITY:

Evaluate the current culture of your practice. What is unique about your practice? What story do you want to tell? Conduct a brainstorming session with your team about what you can do to be different from other dental practices in your community and list action items you will implement each month over the next twelve months to continue to build your culture.

CHAPTER 6

Core Values

N ow that you know the type of vision you are working toward and the culture that will help you get there, it's time to look at the core values necessary for creating that culture. Core values are the rules of the game. They define what your practice stands for and how you will achieve your vision. If you focus on the wrong core values, you could end up with the wrong culture, one that isn't attractive to your ideal customer or those you prefer to hire. This chapter not only explores the importance of core values but also gives strategies for how to make sure your company establishes the right core values for the business you're building and growing.

Why Are Core Values Essential to a Dental Practice?

Core values help form the culture of your practice and enable you to reach your vision. Core values guide every decision you make for your practice. For instance, if one of your core values is "Use the highest-quality materials," then any materials that aren't of the highest quality won't be considered, no matter how affordable they are. If one of your core values is to "Hire and develop the best," then you'll always ensure you're hiring the top people for your practice and not bring in someone who's not qualified to save a few dollars in salary. If one of your core values is "Customer obsession," you'll be fanatical about over-delivering to your patients and with customer service. If you have a team member who is rude to a patient, you won't ignore it or let it slide. You'll likely have gone over expectations on a regular basis and would let them go without multiple warnings because of that.

If you're not clear about your core values, you'll find that you're always making decisions based on changing values or ideas. One month, you may make a purchase because it is the cheapest option. In another month, you may make a purchase because you found the highest-quality option. Those two decisions are based on two different core values. Running an office in this way is likely to produce frustration and a chaotic operation. Knowing and sticking to your core values makes the office run more smoothly.

Another reason core values are essential to your practice is that they can become a calling card for you. When you share your core values with the public, then these core values let your customers know just whom it is they are dealing with and what to expect. For instance, if one of your core values is to "Value patient feedback," your patient will have reasonable expectations that you may be more likely to hear her out when she expresses concern or disappointment than another dental practice that does not include that as a core value would be to listen to her.

You Need to Choose the Right Core Values for Your Practice.

Be careful when identifying your core values. Don't choose core values simply because they sound good or would look good on a plaque on the wall of your waiting area. Be deliberate. Choose core values that are right for your practice because you must be able to live up to them. You must live them. They must become a part of you and your team. When you're doing something fascinating in your practice, it will always be linked back to one of your core values. Your core values are an essential element to defining and building your brand.

Your core values are the heartbeat of your practice. They describe who you are as a practice and what you hold dear. They're about how you relate to team members, patients, and people outside your practice.

We all have personal values, things we won't stand for, and causes we support. So how do you determine those that are the core values of your practice? One way is to get your team involved. It can be helpful to bring in key members of your team to discuss developing your core values. Remember, I said core values must be true to you—they must be authentic. So, don't just make them up or write them down because they seem nice. Identify the values that are already present within your practice and the values that support your vision.

Write all of the values for your practice and create a list. Does this list seem like the right fit? Can these core values stand the test of time? Or will they need to change in a month, six months, or a year? As you read over your list of core values, be sure they resonate with who you are as the leader of your practice and what you see your practice becoming.

If these values seem to support your vision, they can become a framework for your culture.

Show Off Your Core Values.

Your core values should not be a secret! Share them with your patients and the community! Along with your company's vision and mission statements, print and display your core values. Place them in a prominent spot in the office. Point them out to new patients during your office tour. Once your team members are in line with the company's core values, they will strive to give you and your patients their absolute best.

Enlist Your Team to Build Your Core Values.

Very early in our transformation to a Delivering WOW practice, we were working on culture, and I sat down with the team and asked, "What's important to us? How do we want to be known in the community?"

I could have done this on my own, but it would not have been nearly as powerful as involving my team. Getting my employees involved gave them a sense of ownership of the process. In considering what we wanted to be known for, we listed several things.

These are the core values that spoke to the culture of our business:

- Always show compassion. It's important to truly understand our patients' needs and meet them there. We want to treat our patients with kindness and understanding.
- Ask the right questions. It's important for us to be able to listen to understand. Understanding our patients' fears, concerns, and points of resistance helps us to treat them properly and provide better solutions to their problems.
- Deliver a WOW experience every time. Consistency is important.
- Listen with two ears and one heart. The heart in business had to be compassion, love, and understanding.
- Pursue growth and learning. We have weekly lunch-and-learn sessions to ensure we are always learning as a team. All of our team members also have Kindles to read books to help with their personal development.

- Think big and have fun. We are innovative and think creatively. We have a relaxed working environment where we love going to work, and the patients feel it.
- Build a positive team and family spirit. If we aren't working together as a team, then we can't serve our patients to the best of our ability.
- Insist on the highest standards. We want the best for our patients regarding the quality of dentistry that we provide as well as the environment in which we provide it.
- Build a stronger community. We will always make giving back to the community a part of our culture.
- Be humble. As we grow, we want always to remain grateful for what we have and humble in how we carry ourselves.

One of our core values mentioned above is "Pursue growth and learning." Our latest book for our office book club was *Start With Why*, by Simon Sinek. In a recent lunch-and-learn, the team was discussing the book when I walked in. I overheard the discussion. They were comparing Apple and Hewlett-Packard.

They discussed the fact that both companies sell computers, but there is something special about how Apple packages their products. "Apple makes it an experience," Trecia said. "That is the same with our practice. Patients can go to any dental office, but they choose us because of the experience. We are the Apple of dentistry!"

Normally, I would have been there and taking part in the discussion from the start, but I happened to be out that day for parent-teacher conferences. Upon returning, I heard this lively discussion. It was exciting to me, because it was a real example of our core values and culture in action. The team didn't need me around to adhere to our core values. The core values are a part of them.

We knew that by creating these values and living them out every day, we would be successful in achieving our vision to be the leading dental practice known for Delivering WOW. The next key would be in putting in systems for consistency.

You see, once you put in core values and your team understands the why behind them, magic starts to happen. Everyone knows the rules of the game, and your team knows what sort of culture they are part of—a culture of success!

DELIVERING WOW ACTION ACTIVITY:
Evaluate your core values. Are these core values practiced every day in your office? If not, it's time to get your team together and plan! Don't have written core values in place? Brainstorm with your team to create a new set of core values and discuss why each core value is significant.

CHAPTER 7

Team

While all of the six elements of the Delivering WOW experience are essential, your team holds a special place of significance.

Hiring is one of the biggest decisions you will have to make! The types of hires you make will affect your overall business, including how your company delivers on its core values, as well as the culture you develop.

Before we discuss your team, let's consider your role as the leader of your team.

Being a strong leader is critical, because the leader will provide direction and set the tone for the team. Your job as a leader isn't to know all of the answers, but to attract the right people to get the job done. Your responsibility is to inspire your team, to put in tools for their training, and to ensure they know precisely what you want.

Leading Your Team

No matter if you own your practice or are currently working as an associate, the key to having a super productive team who follows systems and delivers WOW is to be a strong leader. Strong leaders are very clear about what's required of the team and aren't afraid to let them know. Strong leaders demand excellence and inspire their team by what they've done for each team member, patient, and the community as a whole. Strong leaders build other leaders.

When you choose to become a Delivering WOW practice, it's important to begin on a path of personal development. Work on growing personally and not just professionally. Turn your car into a driving university as I did to mine. Listen to podcasts, books on Audible, or other educational material as you commute. Join a mastermind group with other dentists who are taking action, such as those in Delivering WOW Platinum Coaching Program, my Inner Circle Mastermind, or something you organize yourself in your local area or online. Hire a coach. I've worked with a coach and am part of a mastermind group to stretch my thinking to the next level, contribute my areas of expertise, and learn from others. Masterminds are also an excellent way to find people to hold you accountable for taking the actions you need to take to fulfill your personal and professional vision and stay true to your mission and core values.

Here are seven key areas to master if you want to become an exceptional leader of your practice:

1. **Communication.** As a leader with a vision, it's imperative that you share your vision, your ideas, and your core values with your team. If you find you're having a hard time getting people to fall

in line with the practice's vision or with an idea you have, it's very likely you aren't communicating as effectively as you can. Inspire your team to see just how phenomenal your practice can be when the patients are WOWed and your business is profitable. Make sure your team understands the benefits of aligning with the company's vision. You'll have a hard time transforming into a WOW practice if you can't communicate this desire and vision.

2. **Commitment.** It's important to commit to your goals, take action, and follow through. To achieve your vision, you might have to make significant changes in how you do business. Because the transition may not be easy, you'll need to be prepared to commit to this new path. It may require adjustments that some on your team, at first, may not embrace. You may even lose some team members who don't share your vision. If you are wishy-washy and can't commit, then your team will see this, and there will be confusion and a lack of interest in following through on the changes. You must lead by example, so your team sees you are in this for the long haul. The Delivering WOW experience starts with you as the leader. You must be willing to stick by the decision you've made no matter what.

3. **Confidence.** Not every day at the practice will be great, no matter how well you plan or how strong your team is. The same is true at home, but strong leaders will persevere. When something goes wrong, don't panic. Be a true leader and create an action plan to get things back on track. Create a new system, and don't be afraid to scrap a system that isn't working in favor of one you believe will work better. A Delivering WOW team will support you when you need it and work extra hard to help your business grow.

4. **Honesty.** Honesty is an essential component of leadership. Once you're honest with your team, they will relate more with you and trust you. For example, many dentists struggle to control expenses, but their team doesn't know it's an issue. Be honest with your team, and they will do their part to help control costs. They'll also grow to trust you more, because honesty inspires trust. If your team is to trust you, your honesty must be evident and consistent. This isn't just about what you say; it's also what you do. What you say and do must match. Being honest will help you build your team, because your team will feel it can trust you to do what you say. Here is a simple way you can show honesty: uphold your promises. If you say you will do something, do it. If you make a mistake or find you can't keep your promise, own up to it.

5. **Decisiveness.** Decisiveness means being able to evaluate a situation and make a decision. While this sounds simple, many people have a hard time with it. They don't want to make a choice, so they keep putting off making a decision or keep going back on decisions. This creates chaos and confusion in your practice. It also makes it difficult for your practice to move forward, because there will be no real commitment to decisions you make, as your team will expect a different decision at some point. If you want to be a good leader, be decisive. Weigh your options before you make a decision, make a decision based on what information you have available, and make the best decision you can given what you know. Don't drag out decisions. This doesn't mean you must make rash choices or snap decisions without proper consideration, but it does mean you should consider the situation, make a decision, and act accordingly.

6. **Intelligence.** If you want to be a good leader, you'll need to show your team you have the mental power to make sound

choices. This doesn't mean you have to be a genius or even the smartest person in the room, but you do need to know how to get information you need to make decisions and have the smarts to put the right people in place to make wise choices themselves in doing what you delegate to them. And that brings us to . . .

7. **Delegation.** As a leader, you must be able to delegate. Many small-business owners, and dentists in particular, are stressed out because they just don't delegate. They feel they must do all the work themselves. That's no way to grow. You can't scale your operation if you refuse to delegate. I understand one of the reasons some of us don't delegate is because we feel no one can do the work how we do it. And that may be true. But it's possible to delegate to someone who can do the job his or her way and also produce an excellent result. You might even find that the person does the task better than you ever could. Delegation is important if you're to be an effective leader because delegating helps you focus on doing the essential tasks that only you *can* do, either because of a licensure issue or because it's an ownership or leadership issue. Once you start to delegate, you'll have more freedom and less stress, because more will get done and everyone will not be counting on you to make every decision.

Creating a WOW Team

When you commit to building a WOW team, you will need to look for people who are a good fit for your practice's culture. Not every applicant will fit into the culture. Individuals who are just looking for a paycheck or who aren't willing to do whatever it takes to get their job done won't be a good fit. The same is true with complainers. In fact, having even one team member with a poor attitude or poor work ethic can put a strain on your practice.

When you commit to becoming a Delivering WOW practice, you're not just looking for ordinary employees. You're looking for star team members. Every team member must be a star and add value. It is vital for you and your team to realize that every position is critical to having the practice achieve its vision. Team members must know that if you did not need certain tasks to be done, then you would have no reason to pay a wage for the tasks to be completed.

Perhaps you already have employees and wonder how they will fit into the Delivering WOW practice you're transforming your business into. The best way to help people who are already a part of your practice make the transition is to involve them in the process. Explain the vision and the transformation you expect to see in the workplace and how it will benefit them. Be sure to show them that you welcome them on the journey. Then create the conditions to help them grow with you so they become WOW team members.

As you redefine your vision, some of your current team members may feel the transformation is too much work for them, and that's okay. Not every person may want to be a part of your vision. I had one lady who said that our transition into a WOW practice would be too much work. I understood her concerns but informed her that it was the new path for the practice, and that I understood if she didn't want to be a part of it. She found another practice that was a better fit for her and moved on. I was a strong leader, and as much as I liked her, I didn't let one team member's resistance influence my decision to redefine my practice. I pressed ahead with all the extremely motivated team members who were ready to WOW.

Here are some key ways you can help your employees become WOW team members:

1. Communicate your vision. Be sure to explain your vision and show your team members how they fit into it. It's important that your team members feel included and see their roles in your new practice. Let them know they're significant to this transformation.

Invest in your team's development. Just as you are growing personally and professionally, so should your team. Facilitate this growth by providing tools and resources. Consider providing Kindles to your team to fast-track their learning. I did this at my office, and it has been amazing to see team members reading my recommended books and excitedly discussing what they learned.

If you need help choosing books, three great team reads are *The Compound Effect* by Darren Hardy, *Eat That Frog!* by Brian Tracy, and *What Got You Here Won't Get You There* by Marshall Goldsmith. If you're new to Audible.com and would like a *free* audio copy of any of these books, you can download one through my partnership with Audible. The link to claim your free book is on the resources page at DeliveringWOW.com/WOWResources.

2. Create team incentives. It's important to incentivize. When you have a WOW team, those team members should feel the benefits that come along with that. Look at ways you can incentivize your team. One way we incentivize team members in our office is by sharing profits with them. I've provided a share of profits to team members as bonuses over and above their regular pay. This way, we all share in the growth of the company. When the team delivers WOW, they get some right back! If you decide to provide a bonus to your team, make sure it's based on profits and not production or collections.

3. Recognize team members. While it can be good to offer monetary incentives your whole team can receive and share in, most times this is not necessary. If you're a great leader and your team shares in your vision, they will perform. I constantly "brag" about my team in front of patients. We also share quite a bit about our team's accomplishments on our social media pages. Some fun things we've done to reward the team are spa days and painting parties. Once, we surprised our team with a shopping spree, after which we met for lunch and they shared what they bought for themselves.

4. If you're creating a WOW team, it's important for team members to know what you expect of them. Be sure to define each person's role and responsibilities in your practice. Don't assume they know what to do or how you want them to do it. Unclear roles and responsibilities are at the heart of many inefficient and ineffective workplaces. Don't let this be the case for yours. When you clearly define and communicate these roles and responsibilities, team members have a better chance of living up to—and exceeding—your expectations.

Many small-business owners, including dentists, believe the salary or wages they provide are a reward or incentive enough for their employees. This is simply not true, and if this is your approach, it's shortsighted and will cost you. Taking care of your employees is an important part of your job when you are a Delivering WOW practice because your employees—your team members—take care of your customers. If you aren't treating your employees well, don't expect them to treat your customers well.

When you take care of your employees and make them feel connected to the vision, they'll give you 100% because they know they're part of the process of growing the business. Compared to unmotivated employees, that 100% effort will feel like 200% or more! Your team members will get excited and happy when they're Delivering WOW. They'll get invested in creating big wins for the practice. When patients come back, your employees will get excited. When goals are met, your employees will feel proud.

A New Approach to Hiring

One of the top ways that we've been able to grow a phenomenal team is by looking at each role in the office and deciding what personality style might be the best fit for that position. For example, we have two ladies who work at our front desk. One is responsible for being the big personality who welcomes every patient when they arrive. She knows details about patients' families and loves to chat with them and make them feel at home. She's the one who has fun with the patients and has no fear asking for video testimonials. The other lady is very detail-oriented. She answers all patient emails and appointment requests very eloquently and quickly and is responsible for going over treatment plans in a systematic way and auditing patient ledgers.

They have two entirely different personality styles, but both are critical to the success of the front office. When filling these positions, we knew which personality styles would be the best fit; we asked candidates to take a personality profile assessment so we could get the best fit. This meant we couldn't hire a quiet, shy person for the extroverted front-desk position, so there was no need to interview that personality style. A shy person wouldn't be a good fit. We also took this approach when hiring an assistant for my high-energy, enthusiastic hygienist. Her assistant needed to have a calm, compassionate personality style to support fearful patients.

One resource I've found helpful is the DISC profile, which was devised by psychologist Dr. William Moulton Marston. It includes four components and measures behavioral styles. It's a personal assessment tool used to analyze behavioral patterns and how they could influence their overall personality at work and at different levels in the career ladder. It also helps people understand behavioral patterns of those with whom we deal in the business world or in day-to-day life.

A DISC profile includes the following components:

1. **Dominance (D)**

   Confidence is the key trait in such a person falling in this category. It is common for these individuals to place a strong emphasis on achievement of results and goal orientation. They can be straightforward and blunt, open toward diversity, and adventurous by nature, accepting any challenging situation coming their way.

2. **Influence (I)**

   These individuals are said to be great natural leaders. They influence others and take charge of situations, but they take everyone along with them. Relationship-oriented and persuasive by nature, these people are very collaborative and see the brighter picture in any situation.

3. **Steadiness (S)**

   Individuals falling into this category are persistent in their behavior. They don't like to be rushed or pushed beyond limits as they exhibit a calm demeanor. They emphasize cooperation, and to a certain extent, they do adjust to unusual circumstances, dealing with things in a subtle manner. They are very supportive of their colleagues and subordinates and are humble and down to earth.

4. **Conscientiousness (C)**

   The name says it all; these individuals are focused on accuracy and quality of work produced along with emphasis on their competencies. They enjoy being trusted and given responsibility as it means for them independence. They are detail-oriented individuals with sound reasoning and expertise. They are perfectionists who dread being wrong.

All of our applicants, as part of their interview process, receive a pre-interview questionnaire and a quick personality profile test so we have a better feel before we offer them an in-office interview. Visit the resources page to get a copy of the questionnaire and personality profile assessment form.

Your Delivering WOW Team Will Help Drive Practice Goals

To grow every year, I create a budget. I do this to track revenue and expenses as well as to track profitability. I do this by setting a revenue goal for the year and then break that down into monthly goals. I then look at all of the services we provide—cleanings, fillings, crowns, whitening, root canals, etc., review how many procedures were done in each category on average for the prior year, and create targets per category that will cause us to reach my revenue goal. My team then puts goals—the number of each service we want to provide monthly—on whiteboards and tracks them daily. When I instituted this, my team told me, "Doc, those numbers look a little high. They're not realistic." But I pushed on. I said, "No, guys, we can do it."

The first month, we met all of the targets except for one. The second month, we met all of our goals. By the third month, we knew we could go even higher. In fact, I saw my office manager erasing the goals and putting in new targets that were twenty-five percent higher than the ones they had called "unrealistic" a few months earlier! Inviting my team to be a part of transforming the practice was amazing, because it incentivized them to try harder at everything they did.

That's the power of making your team feel like an important part of what you're doing. They work to meet and exceed goals, sometimes even setting higher goals themselves.

But building the right team isn't just about meeting and exceeding goals in your practice. Building the right team is also about the feelings of respect and connection that grow. For example, one day I walked into the office and one of my dental assistants said she had a dream about me.

She gave me a hug and said, "I just want to tell you, this is the best job ever. Thank you so much for the opportunity to be part of this team."

Another time, a dental assistant who had seen a Facebook post that we were looking for a dental assistant for our growing practice called every day saying, "I have to be a part of this incredible team!" She was hired and is super committed to our core values and vision. She's been phenomenal.

I'll sometimes put my head around the corner and see a team member giving an arm-and-hand massage to a patient. The team member will look up, and our eyes might connect. We just smile. There's a special bond in this work of WOW. That's the environment we have, and that's the team we have.

Going to work is fun for us. Patients can sense it. They feel it. They tell me this all the time. That's why I can't stop talking about my team. I walked in one day recently, and they had come up with a team vision statement. It was about supporting each other. I love it!

You may have noticed that I refer to my staff as my team. That's because we are a team, working together toward a common goal— which is the fulfillment and maintenance of our shared vision. We have a sense of camaraderie and respect for one another. Consider how you think of your team members and commit to working together to achieve the vision.

Delivering WOW in Action

Dr. Meghna Dassani, DMD
Dassani Dentistry
Houston, Texas
DassaniDentistry.com

I am a general dentist and built a very successful practice. As successful as it was, we didn't have clear systems in place, so our days were often hit or miss. Delivering WOW has helped me systematize my practice, get my whole team working together toward a common vision, and meet or exceed our financial goals, even while working easier—and fewer—work days.

After creating vision boards with my team and discussing how achieving our practice vision could help them accomplish their goals, everyone started working together to achieve that vision. We put systems in place, set KPIs, found training where needed, used Facebook marketing techniques, and implemented WOW elements into our patient experience.

Team morale has been great. Internal referrals from patients have increased, and we have even grown our sleep apnea practice while reducing marketing costs using Anissa's Facebook marketing strategies.

Delivering WOW has us functioning as a well-oiled machine. Everyone knows what they need to do and the numbers we need to reach to achieve our goals, and I'm now free to focus on performing the procedures I love. I now also have the confidence and ability to hire an associate to continue our practice growth.

DELIVERING WOW ACTION ACTIVITY:

Have a close look at your current team, and make sure they are aligned with your vision. If not, have a discussion with them about the importance of having all team members being committed to the vision. If they're not willing to commit, let them know that it is OK to choose another office that might be a better fit.

Subscribe to the Delivering WOW Dental Podcast in iTunes as well as other podcasts to scale up your learning. Download the Audible app to start turning your car into a driving university. Join our free Dental Marketing and Profits Facebook group at DentalMarketingAndProfits.com to mastermind with other top dentists around the world who are taking action to get results. If you're ready to take big action, visit DeliveringWOWPlatinum.com to learn how the Delivering WOW Platinum Coaching Program can help you. You can also consider joining my Inner Circle Mastermind Group, where I work directly with dentists to implement Delivering WOW into their practice!

CHAPTER 8

Systems

Would you be willing to make one single, simple change in your practice if it would guarantee you could regularly meet eighty to ninety percent of your daily revenue goal by lunchtime?

Most likely, you're saying yes to this question. Of course, you'd be willing to make one single, simple change if it could have such a dramatic impact on how much you earn.

Well, that's what this chapter is all about. It's about changing the way you do business so that you get to a more efficient and profitable way of running your practice. The single change: systems.

Many companies lack the proper systems to produce the massive results they want. However, by systematizing your practice, you can boost results and create actionable steps to reach your goals.

Systems also ensure consistency and accuracy and allow all of your team members to know exactly what they must do. Once you have systems, the systems can run the practice, and you can create more time for what matters most or for what you have defined in your personal vision.

Let me give you one example of a single, simple change we made. We created a system for block scheduling. That was the change I mentioned at the start of this chapter that allowed my practice to regularly meet eighty to ninety percent of our daily revenue goal by lunchtime.

Here's the specific block-scheduling plan we used. If you follow these steps, you too will be amazed by your results:

1. Create three morning blocks on your schedule. In my case, they are from 8:00 A.M. to 9:00 A.M., 9:00 am to 10:00 A.M., and 10:00 A.M. to 12:00 P.M.

2. Blocks can only be filled with four or more fillings, a crown, veneers, implants, or a combination of the above. I do not do root canals, but they could be placed in a block as well.

3. Patients requiring a longer block can take the two-hour block from 10:00 A.M. to 12:00 P.M. or two one-hour blocks (8:00 A.M. to 9:00 A.M. and 9:00 A.M. to 10:00 A.M.).

4. Cements, follow-ups, consults, and single fillings are not to be placed in these blocks.

5. One morning of the week and every afternoon are not blocked to accommodate one to three fillings, cements, adjustments, consults, etc.

6. If appointment blocks are free for the next day, they can be released after 1 P.M. If lab cases come in that day, we'll call to schedule those patients in these released spots. Patients love it when they can get back in quickly to cement their cases.

Once we started offering every patient who had four or more fillings or a combination of crowns to do all work in one day, we were amazed at the results. What we heard was, "Of course I'd prefer one visit. Why would I want to come back several times?" That was very interesting and profitable. We also now offer to do treatment on both sides in one visit. Yes, it means patients might be numb on both sides, but we just inform them that it should be back to normal in two to three hours, so they know what to expect. Oral surgeons numb both sides all the time and advise patients what to expect, so we do the same. Our hygienists also offer to do full-mouth scaling and root planing in one visit, and our patients love it, because they don't have to come back to go through the process twice.

This system has been a game-changer for my practice because it allows us to schedule longer, more-detailed procedures in the morning when our eyes are fresh. It provides added convenience to patients, because they no longer have to figure out how to fit multiple dental visits into their busy lives. Block scheduling also decreases overhead costs, because you use fewer setups throughout the day. We reduce the cost of sterilization bags, needles, water, disinfectant, and electricity. This new way of scheduling also lets me work fewer clinical hours. What used to take two and a half hours seeing five patients thirty minutes apart for one filling can now be done in one hour. And it makes it possible to earn eighty to ninety percent of our day's revenue by lunchtime.

Yes, that's one simple change in how we schedule appointments. Creating a block-scheduling system has allowed us to increase our efficiency, revenue, and client satisfaction.

That's the power of a well-placed system.

Why Do We Need Systems?

Systems are essential to delivering a WOW experience. Systems help create consistency so patients can count on the same results and the same experience on every visit. But systems aren't just for creating a consistent experience for patients. Systems help create workplace efficiency so you can get more done in less time and utilize fewer resources.

Implementing systems into your practice may be an intimidating idea for some dentists, but actually understanding the benefits of systems can transform your practice. When I began implementing systems, I started experiencing significant growth. You just can't significantly grow your practice fast if you refuse to implement systems in your practice.

Not every system has to be complicated, and indeed, many of those in our office aren't. Systems are simple, standardized ways of doing things. If there's a problem or breakdown in our office, it's almost always because there was no clarity with the system surrounding it, or there was no system in place at all.

Some of the first things with which I standardized and implemented systems involved creating manuals for all positions, minimum quantity lists to manage inventory and supplies, and written scripts for how we'd answer the telephone, patient emails, and Facebook questions.

Let's explore systems and why you need them in your practice.

Which Systems?

Anytime you have an activity that's repeatable, meaning you will do it over and over again, it should have a system. Some common places where you need systems in your practice are generating new patients, tracking referrals and marketing campaigns, collecting patient feedback, managing supplies, patient follow-up, and the patient experience.

All of these are repeatable activities that lend themselves to systemization.

It becomes inefficient and ineffective to continue to perform these operations in an ad hoc way where there's no consistency. It also leads to inconsistent results, because the lack of standardization of the process can sometimes mean a particular activity is performed a different way each time.

How Do You Implement Systems?

Creating systems and processes to manage the flow of tasks at your office will increase your productivity and reduce costs. You will find many automated systems you can implement that reduce or eliminate the need for deep human involvement. Some systems, such as patient appointment reminders, can be automated through the use of an email or text autoresponder that you set to send a reminder to the patient for a subsequent appointment based on a set trigger, such as a particular period of time before the appointment. Other systems may be activated by certain actions, such as a system to collect customer feedback. Your patient-feedback system may be activated at the end of an appointment, whereby you provide the patient an easy way of providing feedback, and a software solution can handle the rest.

Here Are Some Tips for Implementing Systems in Your Practice:

Create an operations manual with pictures.

Write all of the operations you perform in your office within this handbook. Your operations manual will help ensure that your office is not dependent on any one person. This is important, because if a team member leaves, the institutional knowledge of how to perform a particular set of tasks doesn't leave with them. A new hire can simply pick up a copy of the manual and know exactly what's expected of them and how to perform the required tasks for their position. Once things are written, your office is no longer dependent on your constant presence on a daily basis. You can delegate responsibilities and be assured tasks will be completed according to your standardized manual. Having systems documented in an operations manual also has the benefit of allowing you to have a standardized way of judging employee performance.

The operations manual is an impartial gauge of how each member is doing. If someone isn't performing according to the manual, you can see that. Also, if someone says they're following the manual but not getting the results you expect, it's easy to walk through the process with the person to see where exactly he or she may be missing a step.

Create a Key Performance Indicator, or KPI, chart.

Write what each team member must do daily, weekly, and monthly, and create a chart that can be posted in your office. This KPI chart helps define responsibilities and create a standardized way of keeping track of those responsibilities. KPIs, including charts, contribute to measuring your business's performance in critical areas. Your chart that includes team-member responsibilities can help to see how employees are performing, as well as show what needs to be done, which comes in handy in the event an employee stays out sick, goes on vacation, or leaves your practice.

Use checklists for all tasks.

Checklists ensure there's consistency and clarity for all tasks that must be completed for each position. This means you're providing further standardization of your processes, as each team member will follow the same steps for repeatable tasks. It might seem like a lot of work to use checklists, but checklists allow you to focus on what matters most in the time they save over the long term.

Complete a policies-and-procedures manual.

A policies-and-procedures manual helps to address and answer common and uncommon workplace questions, such as employee leave, opening and closing the office for the day, and more. Often, policies and procedures are not implemented or developed until they become issues. Creating this manual helps you put standard policies and procedures in place before you need them.

The main point to remember about systems is to standardize as much as you can when it comes to repeatable activities you engage in regularly. This takes the guesswork and variability out of your results, creates consistent service, and saves time over the long term.

We even created a system for referrals to give each patient who sends a referral as well as the person being referred ten dollars off a future visit. Once someone refers five or more patients, that person becomes a member of our VIP rewards program and receives five percent off all future visits. This referral program is part of a word-of-mouth-inspired marketing system. When we WOW patients, they go out and evangelize for us. They are out in the community talking about us, which, in turn, brings us more business. Every WOW element we offer is a system for growing. None of our WOWs is an isolated instance. Each is wrapped in a system so we can consistently deliver that WOW to every patient.

When you commit to becoming a Delivering WOW practice, systems can also help you get to the massive growth you seek. Systems help answer the question of, "How do I reach my target?"

For instance, as I mentioned earlier, we track each service we provide and have monthly goals for those services on a whiteboard in our office. Every day, we update the total for each service month-to-date with a red dry-erase marker and compare it with our goal. Once we meet our goal, we change the actual number from red to green. This system also allows us to evaluate our targets mid-month, and if it looks like we may not reach a goal, we change the dynamics of the month by conducting a Facebook promotion or writing an educational piece in a patient newsletter for that particular service.

If you set a target of a revenue goal for the year, you can systematize how to get there by putting into place a system for every service you offer.

That doesn't mean you diagnose anything new or different. It just means that you focus on asking better questions to your patients to determine what they want so that you can provide the solutions they seek. It means your phone scripts are so vibrant that prospective new patients know you're the right dentist to serve them. It means you do whatever it takes to start same-day treatment if the patient is ready, versus putting them off to another day. The whiteboard system holds you accountable for being consistent in your case presentations so that patients will schedule their needed treatment. This one system alone increased our revenue by $20,000 one month!

A System for Getting to Your Patient's Why

When your patient comes to your practice, it is important to understand why they're there. What are they looking for? What is their why, or the deep underlying reason they're at the dentist that day? Are they looking for crowns, or do they want peace of mind that a tooth won't break while on vacation? Are they looking for scaling and root planing, or do they wish to ensure their teeth won't get long or loose? Do they want veneers or teeth whitening, or is it that they want self-confidence? Once you know your patient's why, you can ask better questions to provide solutions to the problems they're really there to solve.

The best way to find your patient's why is to ask open-ended questions, such as, "What is your immediate concern?" "Why is that of concern?" "Which side do you want to do first?" "Would you like to schedule this week or next week?" Notice, none of these questions could be answered with yes or no. Each question would require the patient to give details of what they want and why.

One of the most frequent questions I like to ask is, "What is your resistance?" I ask this when patients say they don't want braces or to do a root canal. When you ask this simple question, people tell you their real story. Perhaps their spouse lost a tooth because they had a root canal and didn't do the crown. If they share that story, you can explain the real reason they lost the tooth. Perhaps they don't want braces because of the look of the metal, not knowing that ceramic brackets are an option. Perhaps, their child is getting married next month and their resources are tied up with funding the event. Perhaps they're moving in two months and don't realize you can complete their crowns in plenty of time before they leave. Once you know your patients' resistances, you can speak to those and answer their questions. Once people have clarity, they can make a decision to move forward and accept your recommended treatment.

Listen to Understand What Patients Want—And Then Deliver It

A good way to find out what your patients want is to ask them. Yes, that's it. Ask and listen. This is a pretty simple approach, but it's also pretty uncommon. Often, as dentists, we believe we know what our patients want, or we try to tell them what they want. Because of that, we deliver what we *think* they want rather than focus on delivering what they *really* want.

How often do we actually listen to understand them? Often, we listen to respond only. The difference is stark. Listening to respond is what we naturally do. We listen, waiting so we can jump in and share our opinions and ideas. Often, we aren't even really listening to what the other person is saying because we're so focused on our own thoughts and formulating our replies. All we care about is the response we will make. As the leader of your dental practice, it's important that you listen, ask a question for clarification, and then respond to their reply.

Have you ever had a patient tell you that they wanted to fix their front tooth, but you can't stop focusing on that bombed-out number nineteen? This happens all the time. It's like going to a clothing store and you want to buy a purple suit, and the salesclerk keeps offering you a blue one, perhaps because she thinks that blue is more practical.

But what she fails to realize is that your favorite color is purple, you're going to a wedding, and you want to make a statement. What she should have done was to sell you the purple suit and ask you if you wanted to get a blue one as well.

The same concept applies to dentistry. Listen to your patient, and you will fix their front tooth as well as the bombed-out molar, and then get referrals to all of their family and friends as well! If you don't listen and just push that bombed-out nineteen, you wouldn't learn your patient was fixing their front tooth to go to their best friend's wedding, and that patient might go somewhere else.

Conduct surveys to learn how you can better serve your patients, and then listen to their desires. Better yet, write out their recommendations and decide if these are things you can easily implement. Placing toothbrushes in the bathroom was one suggestion by a patient. Another patient told us although she likes all of the fancy gourmet teas, she wanted good, old-fashioned Jamaican tea, like Ginger and Cerasee. How easy do you think it was to integrate these requests? It was super easy. And the results? Well, it gave our patients something to talk about and showed that we were listening.

Systems Can Make Sure You're Not Overlooking Something Essential

Here is a real example of why you need systems, even for things that seem obvious. One challenge of living here in Jamaica is that there are often droughts that lead to water restrictions. Many times, the water supply is completely shut off. Because of that, people have water tanks that hold water for their homes or businesses. One day, I was working, and the dental chair completely shut off. I thought, "Okay, that's just very strange."

What I found out shortly after that is that our water tanks had completely emptied! As a result of this, the compressor and suction didn't work. We had to close the business for the rest of the day. We had to have water delivered by a private company to fill up the tank. I have someone who tidies up the office. I assumed he was watching the water levels in the tank. However, as you can tell, no one was checking.

I didn't get upset. I said, "Guys, you know what that means?"

They said, "We need a system."

So, we made a system. Every day during a drought, at 12 o'clock, Mr. David looks into our tank to make sure there's enough water to supply us for the rest of that day and the next day.

In the past, I might have gotten very upset or frustrated because we ran out of water. But I didn't react that way after building a Delivering WOW practice, because I knew it happened because we didn't have a system in place to monitor our water levels.

Assigning Ownership of a System

Decide who will be responsible for implementing your systems. Most times, this shouldn't be the business owner. The team needs clearly defined KPIs, proper training, and deadlines. They also need someone to hold them accountable. But they don't need that to come from the business owner for system implementation. In my practice, the person who holds the team accountable is the office manager, who helps to ensure broken elements of a system get recognized, documented, and addressed.

Set aside time to review your business goals and performance and evaluate whether the systems you've put in place have the impact you desire. Review this with the person you've assigned to own your systems. In my practice, I have a weekly thirty-minute meeting every Monday morning to discuss systems and projects that my office manager is currently overseeing.

I attribute our overall success to the Delivering WOW experience, but I must give special credit to systems. Systems are critical to achieving big results. They can increase your revenue by $20,000 in a month. Just by tracking a system, you can put the focus on that system. I know that it has worked for us.

Testing and Measuring Systems and Processes

Keeping track of your KPIs, systems, and other critical methods of measuring or facilitating growth is essential. If you neglect to keep track of your key performance indicators, systems, and other important methods of measuring and facilitating growth, then you won't know when you're progressing or experiencing a setback. If something isn't working, don't blame your people; create a system. Your training manual should be so detailed that anyone can walk into your business and take over a task with a smooth, consistent transition.

It's critical to know your numbers and understand your profits and losses, which should be documented within your financial system. Your financial system should document your revenue, expenses, and profits. Many teach that profit is what you get to keep after all of your expenses are paid. However, I like to think of it a different way. I like to think of profit first and take my profit first. I pull out a percentage of revenue each week and shift it into a profit account and run my business on the rest. An excellent book on this topic is *Profit First* by Mike Michalowicz. (Mike and I discussed this concept on the Delivering WOW Dental Podcast Episode 18.)

To run a lean business, you also have to think about strategies to increase revenue, such as increasing new-patient numbers and having more patients complete recommended treatment. You also have to look at your expenses.

One of the easiest ways to cut expenses is to look at your supply costs. We used a Google search to cost compare all of the materials that we use in our office with an online supplier. We discovered that we were able to cut supplies by thirty percent. We sent this list to our top supplier, who offered to beat the online supplier's price. We then shifted our printing services and our graphics work to online suppliers. We also decided to look at different labs that would provide excellent quality at a lower cost. One area that we did not cut, however, was our budget for our team.

Are there expenses you are incurring because you don't have a system in place to handle that operation? Cutting costs by using your financial system to evaluate where you are can help you have more profits to grow. Another great tip when purchasing equipment is to ask, "Is this the best price?" Most times it is not, and the salesperson or supplier will reduce the cost to accommodate the sale.

Tips for Testing and Measuring Within Your Practice:

1. Complete and work from monthly budgets. Budgets help you plan expenses. When you work with a budget, you can plan purchases, repairs, and more. A budget also lets you know where you may be paying too much in your business.

2. Set your fees based on desired profit margins, not on what feels right or on what others are charging. When creating your fee schedule, determine what your fixed costs break down to per hour and half hour. This means adding up all utilities, rent, salaries, etc., for the month and dividing that figure by the number of production hours per month. You must also take into account your variable expenses, including dental supplies used and lab costs per procedure. In my practice, we have even broken supply costs down to the amount spent per cotton roll for each procedure. Add the fixed costs per hour or half hour plus the variable costs for each procedure. Then, and only then, should you set your fees. Decide what profit margin you

would like to make, then set your fees. When was the last time you raised your prices? A price increase may be necessary and instantly improves margin.

3. Keep a record of your profit margins and compare them from month to month. This helps you evaluate the growth you are making, as well as the overall health of your dental practice.

4. Track and measure the source for all new patients. Your system for lead generation should allow you to track and measure the leads you have coming into your business. Where are they coming from? What are the best sources for receiving new patients? Are there any sources that used to work but are no longer working?

5. Track your conversion of leads to customers. Getting a steady stream of leads is essential to any business. But converting those leads into new patients who are paying customers is the actual test of how well your offer matches the needs of those you are attracting. So how well are you converting those leads into new patients? Which lead source produces a better conversion rate?

6. Measure key performance indicators for all areas of the company. While there may be many key performance indicators you keep track of, based on goals for each position, there should be a few essential ones you monitor to be sure you are progressing toward your overall goals.

Here are some key financial metric percentages for dental practices:

- Staff salaries (25%–30% of overall budget)
- Lab fees (6%–8% of overall budget)
- Facility (5%–7% of overall budget)
- Dental supplies (5%–8% of overall budget)

- Marketing (5%–7% of overall budget)
- Operating expenses (10%–12% of overall budget)

You can also track the following:
- Number of new patients
- Number of calls received for each procedure vs. the number scheduled
- Number of new patients per referral source—including percentage from existing patients and social media
- Number of procedures completed per service category
- Percentage of treatment plans converted

7. Measure your average dollar sale per patient. How much you earn per patient is a key metric and knowing it can help you grow. Once you know the average dollar sale per patient, you can look for small ways to increase it. These small increases can spell big growth for your business over time. Great ways to increase your average dollar sale are by providing same-day services such as adult and child sealants and fluoride as well as selling products that can add value, such as electronic toothbrushes, fluoride, and water flossers. You should also ask each patient if they want to start today. We are not always able to work in same-day treatment. However, after testing and measuring, we decided to add additional assistants to be able to work in more same-day treatment. These assistants accommodate the setup, patient education, and making of temporaries while I am finishing treatment in the next room.

8. Test and measure every marketing campaign. Testing and measuring your marketing campaigns helps you determine your return on investment. This can help you decide which marketing activities are most effective for you. One you start

measuring and testing, you may find that a commonly accepted marketing activity isn't giving you the results you think it is.

9. Do an analysis of your supply costs quarterly. Analyzing your supply costs on a quarterly basis helps to ensure you are getting the best price. Don't assume that a supplier that was once the best option for you still is. The costs of supplies can change often, so analyzing what you are spending can help you take advantage of price drops.

10. Negotiate with your suppliers. We often assume the stated price is the only price there is. Most times, this is simply not the case. Negotiate with your suppliers to get lower rates or better terms. If you regularly purchase a high volume, for instance, then you may be able to negotiate a volume discount. Or, if you have a history of paying on time, then that may have negotiation leverage that can help you get a better rate or better terms in some way.

11. Know your fixed expenses per hour. Knowing your fixed expenses per hour is important because it can help you determine if you are offering the right services and rates, as well as where you need to make improvements. Knowing fixed expenses can also let you know when it's time to hire, as payroll is often the biggest expense for many dental practices.

12. Know your breakeven point. The breakeven point lets you know when you start to make a profit (or when you're operating at a loss). Your breakeven point is simply the point at which the cost of running your business is equal to the revenue you are bringing into the business. When you are bringing in more revenue than it costs you, you've exceeded the breakeven point and turned a profit. When you're bringing in less revenue than it costs you, then you are operating at a loss. Knowing your breakeven point will influence buying and operating decisions.

When you are looking for massive growth, testing and measuring in these areas is critical. This will provide the information you need to help make decisions about purchases, operations, and more. All of these tested elements should be part of a system.

When you begin standardizing processes and implementing systems, you'll be surprised at just how much duplication of effort you can eliminate, how efficient you can become, and how much more time you will have to dedicate to other tasks.

Delivering WOW in Action

Meghan Darby, DMD
Flint River Dental
Huntsville, Alabama and Meridianville, Alabama
FlintRiverDental.com

After four years in the United States Air Force, I built Flint River Dental into a seven-employee practice. Although my practice had grown in the two years since I built it as a start-up practice, running it had become overwhelming. I even had to return to work the day after my mother passed away to keep up with payroll.

Applying the Delivering WOW principles into my practice was life changing. From developing a vision, culture, and core values to building my team, systems, and brand, Delivering WOW helped me go from overwhelmed to in control. It even helped me expand to two locations, each providing compassionate, nonjudgmental care to our patients and giving back to our communities.

Implementing the systems and processes into our practice has been instrumental in our growth, too. For example, reverse engineering our profits helped us identify and confidently discontinue unprofitable procedures and insurance plans, replacing them with more profitable ones.

Finally, by sharing our great culture and core values on social media, we regularly attract new patients and even attract excellent candidates to fill positions as we've needed to expanded our team. I am now very blessed to have a team that serves selflessly, every day, in our two locations.

I can't imagine where we would be if we hadn't applied the Delivering WOW principles and strategies into our practice.

DELIVERING WOW ACTION ACTIVITY:

Go back over this chapter and consider what you can do now to begin implementing systems. Look at your business. Make a list of all of the systems you want to implement this year and break them down into what you will do each quarter, then each month.

CHAPTER 9

Brand

You've finally decided to book your dream vacation. You're going to Italy! You're excited about the trip and can't wait to get there. With your flight already set, you're ready to book your hotel. You look up a few travel sites to see what's available. The first hotel that catches your eye is a great deal! It actually falls a little below your budget. You start thinking about the extra shopping and sightseeing you can do with the money you'll save. Your mind even begins to drift to the wine tour you would like to take. Then you look at the reviews. The reviews are all two or three stars. The pictures of the hotel are okay but nothing special. Then you move on to the next hotel on the page. This hotel is slightly over your budget but is beautiful and even includes free breakfast and Wi-Fi. You notice that every review is a five-star, and all of the testimonials boast about the incredible location, fantastic service, and phenomenal experience you receive as a guest.

It costs more than the other, but which do you book?

There is a good chance you'd book the more expensive hotel. Why? Because its brand is better. Its photos are welcoming and attractive. The reviews are fantastic. The amenities are exceptional.

That is the power of a brand.

So, what is a brand? A brand is what people say about you when you are not around. As it relates to your business, your brand is all about the stories that people tell their friends and family when they describe your practice. It's not about a business card. It's not about a logo. It's about the emotional connection that people have with your business. Once your practice has a fascinating culture and consistent systems, then the result is that when people talk about your practice, they say "Wow!" "Wow, they see me on time!" "Wow, that was the best experience ever!" "Wow, I didn't even feel the injection!" "Wow, they give to charity!" "Wow, Wow, Wow!"

Having a great brand means that people can't stop talking about your business. It means that you have "raving fans." Having a remarkable brand where people can't stop talking about you means you have climbed to the top of the ladder. No company that has a phenomenal brand got there by accident. They all started by creating a vision and by focusing not on the competition but on being unique. They all described their company story through their culture, developed their core values, invested in their team, and made sure that systems were put in place.

Many small-business owners believe the price is the determining factor in customers' decisions, and that's most often not the case. While the price may be a factor, it's often not the deciding factor. As I showed in the example that started this chapter, we often are looking for certain signals and cues about a business, to determine if we will spend money there. Those signals and cues are conveyed in the brand. If the brand fascinates, we'll spend money, even if we could get a lower price somewhere else.

Competing on price is never a winning proposition when you are in business. That's because you can always find someone who is willing to do a task for less. So, if you keep driving your price down to compete, you could very well find that it costs you more to deliver the service than you earn from selling it!

A better way to stand out is by creating a fascinating brand. When you create an exciting brand, you create a consistent promise to deliver a WOW experience and then deliver that WOW experience, so people leave five-star reviews for your practice while sending all their friends and family to you. That means just going through the motions and being like every other practice won't do for you. You want more. You want to thrive; you want to fascinate! Delivering WOW may take a bit more work in the beginning as you change your thinking and transform your practice, but it will pay off with higher returns. Once your brand is known for Delivering WOW, your practice will be on autopilot and can run without you. You'll have more time, you'll earn more money, and you'll have more freedom!

Your dental practice already has a brand; every business does. But that brand may be ordinary and unremarkable before you make the Delivering WOW transformation. If you find your brand is weak or nondescript right now, don't be discouraged. Many of us have been there. We weren't taught how to build strong brands when we were in dental school. But as we realize we want our practices to be better than they have been, we realize we must do something different!

When you have a WOW brand, you'll find you attract more customers and don't have to compete solely on price. You get to compete on your Delivering WOW point of distinction.

So, what does it mean to have a WOW brand, and how do the other elements of the Delivering WOW experience contribute to that brand?

Let's find out.

What Is A Delivering WOW Brand?

While I'm speaking specifically to dentists in this book, a Delivering WOW brand is something any service business can aspire to have, regardless of industry or niche. A Delivering WOW brand is a brand that promises to fascinate its customers through a phenomenal experience.

In the context of your practice, what does Delivering WOW mean? I've already shared with you what it means in my practice: It's about intentionally being different and creating stories for our patients to share. It's about the details of the office tour, music, and headphones to take away the sound, hand-and-arm massages to relax patients before treatment, and unexpected surprises, such as hot chocolate for the kids and perfume in the bathroom. It's about calling our patients after treatment and on their birthdays. We even have a "Kids Club" where children are treated to their own newsletter, T-shirts, and water bottles.

These amenities are just some of the features that help contribute to our WOW brand. As you've just read in the chapter on systems, there are also many invisible features that also contribute to our brand. A great example is the process that we take patients through from the first phone call to when we ask them for a video testimonial or a review. (Our tight system ensures that they will say "WOW!")

Everything you do in your business contributes to your brand. If you think the alginate on the floor from your last patient in your waiting area doesn't matter, you're wrong. If you think it doesn't matter that your receptionist doesn't make eye contact and smile, you're wrong. If you think it doesn't matter that you never seem to have tissue in the restroom, you're wrong. Each of these may look like a little thing when the pressure to do so much overwhelms you, but each can take away from the brand you are building.

How the Other Delivering WOW Elements Contribute to Your Brand

As mentioned earlier, your brand is what people say about you when you're not around. Building a fascinating brand does not just happen. It is a result of successfully mastering every step along the way.

Here is how the other elements in the Delivering WOW experience contribute to your brand:

Culture is the story that you want to tell the world about your practice. It's made up of how you and your team interact with each other and your patients, the core values you hold, and how you present yourself to the community. Culture influences your brand, because if you get it right, you are telling the world what you want your brand to represent.

Core values are the rules of the game of how you develop your brand and ultimately your vision. Core values influence your brand, because they align you with patients who believe in your values. They connect you with your ideal patient.

Team is how your core values will be carried out. It brings the personality to your practice. The team you have interacting with patients will influence your brand, because those interactions will determine the quality of the experience customers have with you.

Systems are what allow you to be consistent in delivering your core values. Systems influence your brand; without consistency, none of your new strategies for growing your brand will stick. You may try something new and get super excited but never follow through.

And of course, your vision clearly defines what the ultimate goal is for the practice and creating a fascinating brand where you have a practice full of "raving fans" is how you will achieve it.

One night, I was relaxing at home with my husband when a message came to my phone from Melissa, my office manager, that a patient had tagged us in his Twitter post. Once I opened the link in the tweet, I saw that it was to a blog article that he had written about his experience in our practice. All I could say was WOW! You never realize the importance of every small detail you put into creating an incredible patient experience until you receive something like this from one of your patients.

Although a bit long, I want to share this blog post by Andre O. Brown (andreobrown.com) in its entirety, as it was at that moment that I knew we had a magical brand.

Good customer service is always appreciated, and in some lines of business, it may make or break you. A good restaurant can get by with great food, but add good customer service, and you'll keep customers coming back. Maybe great service aids digestion. We also like receiving good customer service at stores, at the spa, and at hotels. After all, those are service-oriented establishments, aren't they?

Generally speaking, a good customer experience enhances the delivery of many services. However, there are some areas where we don't expect good service, and if we do receive it, then it's a noticeable exception. When we're sick, we visit the doctor, but whether or not the doctor has a great bedside manner does little to prevent our visit. After all, we aren't going to curl up and die because we don't like how our doctor talks to us. We also expect a long wait and generally accept this as par for the course in the health industry.

We've talked about food and healthcare, both of which we cannot do without. But what about a service that we need but that we generally don't like and tend to avoid for as long as possible? Ever had a toothache? They don't usually start out chronic, do they? However, most of us delay our visits to the dentist until we can't even scream in agony, as the air hitting our teeth would cause further pain.

Visiting the dentist is a uniquely uncomfortable experience. No one likes being prodded and poked in the mouth with drills and pointed metal instruments. And let's not even get started on the scratching and scraping sounds that give a new meaning to the phrase "setting your teeth on edge." Yet, routinely subjecting ourselves to dental procedures can save us a world of pain. However, that's seldom incentive enough for some of us. Is there anything that could make a dental visit bearable? Believe it or not, one dental practice came up with a brilliant approach.

The Jamaica Cosmetic Dental Services (JCDS) Facebook page tries to lure customers with the promise of a short wait time and "WOW experiences." Generally, we expect to wait when we visit the dentist and rightfully use the time to steel ourselves in preparation for the assault against our mouths. However, if you've ever tried to slip a dental visit in on your lunch break, then you know the frustration of long wait periods. So, the promise of a fifteen-minute or shorter wait is good bait.

Before visiting anywhere, a little research is in order. A quick trip to the JCDS website gives you reason for pause. On the site, you are greeted by the smiling faces of JCDS staff members. The image is reminiscent of sitting back in your dentist's chair, minus the bright white light and gnarly instruments. The image is actually quite pleasant and sets the tone for a visit even before you've decided to go.

Once you've entered the JCDS website, you are greeted by photos not of teeth, tools, or office furniture, but of smiling staff members, children, and community outreach programs.

The staff photo in which staff members pose with random things from around the office is worth special mention. One staff member is holding up a sign that says "I love my job," which while unusual is immediately believable because of the sheer fun nature of the photo. These people actually look like they love their jobs!

Another thing stood out on the site: the details of the promise of a "WOW experience." Part of this experience is the promise of a hand massage to relax you before, and music to distract you during, your treatment. By this point, it becomes obvious that these people get something that everyone else has missed: getting people to do something that they don't want to do is possible if you can make the overall experience better. Air travel sucks, but friendly flight attendants can make being stuck in a metal tube for hours slightly more bearable. And no one likes to be reminded that their airplane could fall out of the sky, but fun safety instructions go a long way to making you pay attention. So too, JCDS promises to transform your dental visit with excellent service, and they deliver on this promise!

Getting people to do something that they don't want to do is possible if you can make the overall experience better.

The first thing you'll notice when you visit their office is, well, their office. It doesn't feel like a regular dental office. It's spacious and bright. The treatment areas don't have doors, but still maintain privacy while getting rid of annoying door slamming. The usual dental charts are replaced with large, beautiful portraits of people. In such a beautiful environment, even the tools look less daunting. And if you're a tea drinker, you will appreciate the gourmet tea in the waiting area. Oh, and there is coffee if you fancy that.

As a new client, instead of being greeted by forms to fill out, your receptionist asks you for basic information and enters it directly into the system. That made registration quick and easy! And you'd better drink your lovely tea quickly, because they do deliver on the promise of the 15-minute or less wait time.

Your first visit starts with a tour of the facility. That's right, a tour. They do everything to distract you from what you're actually there to do. And guess what, it works! After the tour, you're taken to the treatment room and talked through your treatment.

One thing that stands out as you interact and speak with the staff is their attentiveness—they seem truly interested in your comfort and well-being, not just in getting the job done. One way that they ensure that you're relaxed and comfortable is by offering you a complimentary hand massage before you start your treatment. But wait, there is more! For many people, the noise of the machines and instruments in their mouth is even more nerve racking than the actual feel of the instruments. Understanding this and having a desire to make you as comfortable as possible throughout your procedure, the brilliant minds behind JCDS came up with another great distraction. You can listen to music of your choosing, delivered to your ears via headphones throughout your treatment. The relaxing effect of this is not to be underestimated.

After your examination and treatment, you are offered a warm towel. Only after you are comfortably clean does your dentist or an assistant explain what was done and make recommendations for other procedures. Most places stop there. JCDS takes this a step further and prepares a treatment plan that is printed and provided to you before you leave.

On the counter by the reception area is a collection of small signs, including the "I love my job" sign featured in the photo on the website. Nestled in this pile is one sign that epitomizes the experience promised and delivered by JCDS. That sign reads: "We treat people, not teeth." That sentence is what truly distinguishes the JCDS experience: they focus not on your cavities, your cleaning, your crown, nor your filling. Instead, they focus on you, and everything else falls into place.

It is evident that much thought was put into how to transform a normally unpleasant experience into one that you no longer dread. From your first contact online to your first visit to the office, the overall experience created by JCDS is actually enjoyable, and that is quite a feat.

I am very honored that Mr. Brown took the time to share his experience with others. It touches me in a special way to know that all of the work that we are doing is making a difference. His feedback makes my work worthwhile. It shows that what we do really matters.

Create Marketing to Attract Your Ideal Patients

Marketing is about being remarkable. What makes you different? I see so many dentists place Yellow Pages and newspaper ads that list all of the services they offer. They say we do cleanings, crowns, extractions, dentures, etc. Well, these are services that most dentists are known for providing. Make sure to be known for more than the services you offer.

Make your ads remarkable! In our print and digital advertising, we discuss our on-time guarantee and that we offer complimentary hand massages. You may think a hand massage would not attract patients. Let me tell you, it does. Another great example of a practice that gets it right is that of orthodontist Dr. Ann Marie Gorczyca. She has a Summer Splash party for her community each year. Everybody knows her practice for that party. People look forward to it the entire year. And guess what? It has nothing to do with Orthodontics.

The way you market plays a role in the brand you build. If your marketing is always about being the low-price option, then you will attract patients who are looking for the lowest price. If your marketing is about changing lives through beautifying people's smiles, then you will attract lots of people who want to improve their smile. If your marketing is about Delivering WOW experiences, then you will attract people who are fearful or appreciate paying a little extra to be treated like a VIP.

That brings me to Ms. Williams, a patient I've had for more than a decade. Ms. Williams has Sjogren's syndrome and takes three buses to get to our office. She's a retired teacher with no insurance. She doesn't have a lot of money, but she knew she had a problem, because her teeth kept getting cavities. Frustrated, she came to my practice after seeing me on a morning show. Upon evaluation, I realized she needed a ton of work. Really just about every tooth needed a crown. We segmented her treatment, and she saved and did one or two crowns at a time.

We're definitely not the least expensive dental practice in town, but she still chose to come. One day I asked her, "Why is it that you choose to come to us? You must pass ten to fifteen dentists before reaching our office."

Her response: "I just love the way you make me feel!"

I'm happy to report that all of Ms. Williams' crowns have been completed. We chose to help her a little along the way, but she was committed because of the patient experience.

Build your marketing around sharing your core values. Focus on your culture and all of the fun that happens behind the scenes. Create the story that will become your brand.

By the way, you don't need a large marketing budget to get results, thanks to the array of marketing options we have available to us today. Marketing costs have gone way down due to the use of the internet and other creative strategies. In the early part of this book, I shared some numbers with you: we were able to get 250 new patients in one month with one strategy. In another example, we saw a 1,500 percent return on an ad. Some marketing strategies are winners. By tracking your return on investment, you'll double your efforts on the winners and eliminate the losers.

While there are many ways of marketing your practice, I will discuss some of my favorites here. They are charity, host/beneficiary arrangements, strategic alliances, social media (especially Facebook), and dental-marketing funnels. Because funnels and some other marketing tactics are big topics, I've also created a bonus chapter dedicated to help you build your brand and practice through dental-marketing funnels after working through the basics of Delivering WOW. In this chapter, I'll help you build through host/beneficiary arrangements and strategic alliances.

The Little-Known Secret to Building a Fascinating Brand

Are you ready to skyrocket your brand? I mean take it to a whole different dimension? I will share with you the one thing that has catapulted my happiness and my brand. This one thing has connected me to more people and allowed people in my community to view my practice in a whole new way.

It's not the on-time guarantee; it's not the perfume in the bathroom. It's not even the dentistry. The one thing that has set us apart in our community is our serious commitment to charity. In fact, our number-one focus for one year was on our community impact. If you choose to focus on building stronger communities, you'll quickly become a community leader and distinguish your brand.

By supporting people in need, you not only help the community, but you also help yourself. In our case, we support a different charity each month. Service has always been close to my heart, as I've been volunteering and supporting causes since high school. Paying it forward and making a difference in the lives of others can only lead to happiness, and I have experienced that the more that I give, the more I receive. Giving back through my business, where I can support some of the community's neediest residents, involves the team and allows us to change lives.

A few years ago, we created Project Smile, our free smile makeover competition. We used social media to promote the contest and were overwhelmed by the sheer number of entries that came into our contest email inbox. People shared a photo of their smile and shared their stories of why we should choose them. We then selected three finalists, who came into the office to get a complimentary cleaning, exam and x-rays, and then we selected a winner.

The year 2013 was a particularly challenging year for us to choose a winner. One entrant was a teacher on a fixed and very limited income. She was missing her lower front teeth and was extremely embarrassed because her students were always questioning her about why her smile "looked like that." Another finalist was a lady who was literally begging and crying because her self-esteem was low. She opened her mouth and showed that she was missing her front tooth. The last finalist was a high school student who was born with cleft palate. He came in with his mother, and they were both excited that he might get the opportunity to finally "look normal."

We were so touched by the three applicants that we chose all three. Genuine tears of happiness and joy were shed by all at the completion of their treatment. Giving back, through my gift of dentistry, as well as choosing all three candidates, was one of the best decisions that I ever made in my career as a dentist. In making a choice to give, people in the community took notice of us, and we started to receive.

If you're like me, there's some likelihood you became a dentist because you have a strong desire to help others, but in the stressed-out, overworked environment many of us find ourselves in, you soon lost sight of why you got into this profession. If that's you, I encourage you to find a way to get back to this. You don't have to do what I do and support a different charity each month but do something that connects your practice to the reason you got into the profession.

There are so many ways we can all help and do charity in the world. Find a way that is close to your heart and do it. Having a dental practice that is involved in charity helps you WOW customers and your community and makes your practice unique.

While giving back makes you feel good on the inside and helps those you are serving, it also has the added benefit of growing your brand.

Host/Beneficiary Arrangements Provide Credibility and Boost Your Marketing

Many dentists think you need to spend a lot on marketing. In fact, I hear so many dentists and entrepreneurs in general say that you have to spend money to make money. However, there are some times when that rule does not apply. And honestly, these are the rules that I want to play by. This one strategy that I will lay out for you has allowed me to build partnerships with top companies in my community, reach out to my ideal patients, and become twenty-eight percent more profitable. This one marketing strategy that I discovered a while back that has helped me to boost my brand is the Host/Beneficiary arrangement.

The Host/Beneficiary arrangement is an advanced marketing strategy where your company teams up with a more established or bigger business in your area that serves an audience that is similar to your own.

The basic way it works is this: You offer a free or deeply discounted offer to customers of the larger organization. The larger organization (the host) shares this offer with its customers. You (the beneficiary) get the implied endorsement of the host.

In the business world, how this works is that you research companies in your area that have customers who would also be ideal customers to your business. You approach the company and create a great free (or discounted) offer that you would like for them to share with clients.

If the company likes your quality and finds the offer useful, there is a good chance it will agree to the arrangement. So why would this bigger company agree to promote your business? Because it's a no-cost way to provide something of value to its customers. The host company doesn't have to pay for the perk you give. You offer it at no cost to the organization.

I decided to apply this advanced strategy to my dental practice, and instead of offering a perk or promotion to its customers, I offered it to their teams.

This is how it looked in my practice: We created an email that included an offer of fifty percent off dental cleanings and shared it with the biggest bank in the country. The email stated that because we believe in building communities and building strong teams, we have decided to create this partnership. The employees were free to use their insurance and share the offer with their friends and family. The offer was for a limited time of one month. Well, needless to say, we were WOWed.

That month, we had over 250 new patients, and our revenue shot up twenty-eight percent from the previous month. We had to hire an additional hygienist because of the rapid growth!

We attribute the success of this campaign to the great offer as well as to the fact that the team's company shared it. Incidentally, even though we offered a promotional price, more than fifty percent of the patients added on additional same-day services such as adult sealants, fluoride, and fillings, and scheduled for future treatment.

Because of our culture of Delivering WOW, after receiving unexpected bonuses such as a complimentary arm-and-hand massage, a full office tour, and an iPad and headphones to take away the sound, they became raving fans.

Because of the success of this campaign, we now create host/ beneficiaries for cleanings with one large and one small company every month. We also offer it to the team of the charity that we are supporting that month.

So perhaps your next question is, "How do I set up these host/ beneficiaries?" Well, sometimes it's all about the relationships. The easiest way to "get through" is to ask a patient who works at the company to make the connection. You can also "cold call," but you might not get one hundred percent agreeing to the partnership. However, even if the acceptance rate is twenty percent, that is quite fine, because there are limitless options of companies that can be contacted. I would suggest making the offer for them to share with their team instead of their customers because this gives them an opportunity to look like a winner to their employees, so they'll be more likely to share your program. Remember, this is a task that can be delegated.

This strategy speaks to what a new patient is worth. You see, it didn't cost more than an email to create and market the campaign. It cost us a little chair time and some prophy paste. But the value of that campaign will last a lifetime!

Does this ever happen to you? At the supermarket or the mall, someone asks you what you do; you tell them that you're a dentist, and they start pouring out stories. After talking about of the problems they have with their teeth and what work needs to be done, they say that they wish they could go to the dentist, but they don't have any insurance. They might even ask you if you offer a discount. What they're really saying is, "How can I afford dental care? Show me how I can afford dental care." Host/beneficiary arrangements can help here as I share in the story below.

In fact, you can get some of your best patients when you meet people in a restaurant, at your kid's school, or even in a parking lot. They want to know how you can make it easy for them to receive treatment.

Recently, I was at a leading hardware store, and the topic came up that I was a dentist. The man asked if I could give him a "discount." I told him I could do something for his entire company. I said I could make a special offer for them all to come in for cleanings for the next month for fifty percent off!"

"Wow, you would do that?" he asked.

"Of course." I then asked him to provide me with the details of the person at the hardware store who could share the offer with the team, and he did just that.

Offering a special promotion for his company was an excellent way for me to get in front of *all* of the employees of the company and help him out at the same time.

Getting these patients in for the first visit is just the first step. You want to make sure you have a system in place to offer extended payment plans with a third party so if they need extend treatment over time, they'll be able to take advantage of flexible monthly payments. For procedures over a certain dollar amount, you could also offer a five percent pre-payment courtesy if they schedule that month and an additional five percent if they pre-pay for their treatment. (Of course, this takes into account that you have set your fees accordingly to accommodate everyone taking advantage of this offer.)

Strategic Alliances Help Grow Your Reach

Another great way to build your brand and grow your practice is through strategic alliances. Strategic alliances allow you to gain access to people and resources you may not otherwise be able to access.

In a strategic alliance, you team up with another business or organization to do a project or certain initiative together. You agree to share resources so you can both gain access to whatever resources you feel you cannot get alone.

For instance, you might develop a strategic alliance with a bridal shop. You might offer a fifty percent discount on teeth whitening to all brides who schedule an appointment and mention the postcard or flyer they got from the bridal shop. The bridal shop gets to offer brides a substantially discounted gift in the form of teeth whitening. You get the opportunity to land a new customer. The bride gets the chance to put on her best smile for her special day.

Teaming up in this way with a bridal shop is a perfect fit for your dental practice, as brides are often in the market for cosmetic dentistry.

Another alliance that we set up was with a top local sushi restaurant. They designed an electronic coupon for a free dessert for our patients to receive during their birthday month. We include this "gift" to our patients with the auto responder that goes out to our patients on their birthdays. It is a win-win-win. Our patients get a gift; the restaurant gets more customers, and we can add value to our patients without paying a thing.

You can get creative when considering strategic alliances. Look at what you can provide to the other side and what you expect to receive. It's important that both sides are receiving value; otherwise, the alliance will not work.

A strategic alliance can help you to grow your practice in a significant way as you gain new customers, resources, and other benefits of joining forces with another organization.

Delivering WOW Creates Raving Fans

Once you have your WOW culture in place and the systems to ensure that there is consistency, then you are well on your way to creating your fascinating brand.

When your patients are WOWed, whether by the amazing dentistry that you provide or how you make them feel, they will want to tell the world. I'm sure you've been a raving fan of another company at some point or another. What is that one thing that they did to captivate you? This feeling of captivation with your practice is what you want your patients to feel.

When you deliver on your promise of WOW, you will find that patients will be so thrilled that they want the people who matter most to them to experience the same joy.

So, get all the other Delivering WOW elements in order, use these marketing strategies to turbo charge your promotional efforts, and be prepared to ignite!

Be sure to do what we discussed in Chapter 8, and that is to listen to understand. Listen to what your patients are saying and what they want. Why are they choosing you? Remember that all the work of Delivering WOW is not about you; it's about your patient. Provide tremendous value, and you'll get massive results.

People buy what they want, not what they need. Find out what your patients want, and then give that to them!

Some spend thousands on ineffective marketing, such as phone-book ads that no longer work. You don't want to do that. Test and measure your marketing efforts, so you know what actually works for you.

Make sure to keep in regular contact with your patients through monthly newsletters and promotions. And be sure that your website is current and has opt-ins for you to follow up with prospective customers as well as a Facebook pixel so that your practice will stay at the top of their minds. This way, WOW isn't a one-time event, but an ongoing activity.

DELIVERING WOW ACTION ACTIVITY:

Evaluate your brand. What does your brand say when you are not around? Is it fascinating? Ask your team, you friends, and your patients how they would describe your brand. Look at the responses. Is it aligned with your brand story? If not, create a list of what you can do to make that change.

CHAPTER 10

Using Facebook to Grow Your Practice

Social media marketing has transformed dental practices in an almost unprecedented fashion. My team and I have spent years studying, testing, and analyzing the best strategies for using social media for dental practices.

At first, we used Facebook to build an audience of over 50,000 raving fans for *my* dental practice and turn those leads into dozens of new patients every month, all by utilizing the best social media marketing techniques available on Facebook to share our story and build great connections with our Facebook fans and with people who had never heard of us.

It wasn't always that easy for me, though. Before I discovered the power of Facebook to build my practice, I spent a lot of money using traditional ways. I had an ad in the phone book, but when I tracked how many patients were coming in, I realized I was only getting two to five patients a month from that. I was barely breaking even on those ads.

I then tested a newspaper ad, running a full-color, *high-converting*, full-page ad that I had commissioned from an award-winning graphic artist. I placed it at the front of the publication on the right-hand side and told the newspaper representative that, "If I get good results, I will continue to use this strategy." I did get a positive return, but it wasn't worth being out the $800 I spent on the ad while I waited to recoup the spend plus a small return.

When we first discovered the power of Facebook for dentists, we were shocked at how fast, flexible, and cost-effective it was. I was still early in learning Facebook, but we were seeing returns of up to 1,500% on my money. That meant for every dollar I spent, I got up to fifteen dollars back! Better yet, Facebook even had *free* ways to grow my practice that helped me get even *greater* returns.

When we realized how much better Facebook was at building our brands and getting new patients in the chair, I couldn't move my advertising dollars from the phone book and newspaper ad to Facebook fast enough.

After testing and refining our strategies, we started experiencing returns of up to 5,000 percent using Facebook, getting fifty dollars back for every dollar we invested on Facebook. Some of our favorite *benefits of Facebook marketing for dentists* include these:

- Facebook gives the most robust ad-targeting capabilities out of all dental social media marketing options.

- Dental Facebook marketing costs less than traditional marketing and other social media for dentists.
- Facebook makes available to everyone the same tools that only big companies used to be able to afford.
- Facebook allows you to act fast to fill last-minute cancelations or promote an event or special offer, getting organic and paid posts up in minutes.
- Facebook gives dentists sophisticated performance data for all Facebook ads they post so you can know your exact return on investment.
- Facebook allows you to change different variations of the same dental Facebook ad to split-test ads against each other.
- And more . . .

Because of how powerful Facebook can be to build a dental practice, my team and I now use the same strategies we used to grow *my* practice to help *other* dentists and dental practices as part of our dental-marketing services.

The strategies we use for our dental-marketing clients are the same strategies I share with you right here and work for dental practices of all shapes, sizes, locations, and specialties. These strategies can help you create a Facebook marketing and organic presence that is effective, efficient, and predictable—no matter what your practice looks like.

Don't worry if you've tried using Facebook to promote your dental practice before, don't understand how Facebook can help grow a dental practice, don't think you have the time for dental Facebook marketing, or think Facebook is expensive. You're not alone. Many dentists feel this way about using Facebook, but I assure you, each of those objections can be overcome, and I'll show you exactly what to do to help you get reliable, affordable, and consistent using Facebook to grow your dental practice.

Whether your practice has been open for decades, is still months from opening, or anything in between, you can use Facebook marketing to grow your practice and get patients in your chair for a fraction of what you'd have to spend on traditional dental-marketing techniques.

The Best Dental Facebook Marketing Techniques to Build Your Practice

This chapter will walk you through the three things my team and I do to build Facebook marketing campaigns for dentists around the world to help you do the same for your dental practice.

First, I'll share the most important things you can do to build a dental Facebook page. The best dental Facebook pages have a few things in common. We'll share what makes the best pages so great, and how you can do the same! If your dental office's Facebook page is bland and ineffective, this section will help you give it life and get it ready to build fans and convert them to new patients. If you're a dentist looking to build an individual presence on Facebook, this section will give you tips to build a great dentist's Facebook page to build your individual reputation and following.

Second, I'll share the best strategies for creating great Facebook posts. Creating social media posts for dentists is one of the favorite things my team does. I'll share the best strategies for creating posts that will help you build a group of raving Facebook fans!

Third, I'll help you plan and prepare the most effective Facebook ads. Facebook advertising for dentists allows you to reach people with unprecedented precision to help you get better *and faster* results at a *fraction* of what dentists and dental practices typically spend on dental ads in traditional media and other advertising. I'll teach you how the best Facebook ads for dentists perform and how you can get the most effective Facebook dental ads strategies working for you.

If you're ready to have the best social media marketing strategies for dentists working on your behalf to build the best Facebook page possible for your practice, the best posts building engagement and raving fans, and the most efficient and effective Facebook ads directing people to your special offers and dental-marketing funnels, then follow the steps I outline in the rest of this definitive guide to dental Facebook marketing!

How to Build the Best Dental Facebook Presence for Your Practice

Every dental practice needs a Facebook page to act as their home base on Facebook and give them a platform to grow and connect with their patients, prospects, and Facebook fans. Here's everything you need to know to build and optimize a Facebook page for your practice even if you haven't opened the doors yet.

Building Your Dental Facebook Page

If you haven't set up a Facebook page, it might help you to know that the process is free and simple. So, if you're just getting started, don't worry. The best dental Facebook pages all got started by following the same simple, five-step process. For an interactive guide to this chapter, including images and links to additional resources to help walk you through the process visually, go to the resources page DeliveringWOW. com/WOWResources or DeliveringWOW.com/Facebook-For-Dentists.

To set up the best dental Facebook page for your practice, you first need to go to the Facebook page-creation page (Facebook.com/Pages/Create). That's a page on Facebook where you create the page and then walk through steps that Facebook guides you through to enter information about your practice. For practice type, most dental offices will select the "Local Business or Place" option on that page.

After choosing the right option for your dental practice, enter your business category and practice's contact information. Common options for business categories for dentists include "Dentist & Dental Office," "General Dentist," "Cosmetic Dentist," and "Pediatric Dentist."

After the initial setup, you will next need to upload an appropriate Facebook page profile picture and cover photo. I suggest using a high-resolution, professional close-up photo of you for a profile picture if you're building a dentist Facebook page, or of your logo if you're building a dental practice Facebook page. Make sure your images are the ideal size for Facebook pages, which change from time to time. Any quality graphic designer or dental-marketing company will know the right size for a Facebook profile picture and cover image.

The best dental Facebook pages also have robust, custom profiles. Specifically, when you are setting up your Facebook page, Facebook will ask you to enter a short description of your practice. Enter a couple of sentences to tell people what your practice is all about. Let them know why your practice is different. You will also be asked to enter hours of operation, team members, and links to your website. Fill out all the demographic and contact information possible.

You can also customize a button under your Facebook cover photo. By default, this is usually set to read "send message" and lets people message you on Facebook. You can change it to a number of things. For dentists, I usually suggest editing the button to allow people to schedule an appointment, start a Facebook Messenger chat, or learn more about your practice, but if you're building dental-marketing funnels, which I'll talk about in Chapter 13, then you can also change it to send people to your dental-marketing funnel to supercharge your Facebook marketing. You can also include links to your website or a dental-marketing funnel in your *about* section.

How to Optimize a Dental Facebook Page

If you already set up your new dental practice Facebook page, congratulations! You're ready to begin posting and promoting your page.

If you already have a Facebook page for your practice, make sure your profile includes all the elements on this page and the additional tips for effectively using Facebook for dentists. Specifically, to optimize an existing dental Facebook page, make sure:

- Your dental Facebook page has complete practice contact information.
- Your page has accurate hours of operation.
- Your profile picture and cover images are professional, high-resolution images that convey your practice's culture.
- Your *about* section includes complete and accurate statements about what makes your dental practice different.
- You add trusted team members to your dental office Facebook page's list of team members.
- Your button under your Facebook page cover photo directs people to engage with your dental practice in a way you want them to, such as to send you a message or schedule an appointment.

With these things in place, your dental office's Facebook page will be ready for posts and promotion so you can build a loyal audience and attract new patients.

How to Grow Your Dental Office Facebook Page Following

Once your office's Facebook page is set up and optimized, you're ready to build your Facebook following and convert strangers into patients. The first thing you can do to start building your Facebook page following is invite your Facebook friends to like your page. To invite your Facebook friends to like your page, click the gray button with three dots on it under your Facebook page cover photo, to the left of your blue "Learn More," "Schedule an Appointment," or "Send Message" button. Next, click "Invite Friends," and click the "Invite" button next to all friends you want to invite.

This is a quick and easy way to get your first one hundred or more Facebook fans. Although many of these people won't be patients, they will be family and friends who know, like, and trust you; and your invitation to like your page might help you get some of them to become patients. Even if it doesn't encourage them to become your patients, they *will* be likely to like, comment on, or share your posts when they appear in their timeline, thus increasing the odds of your posts going viral! When your patients come in, you can also ask them to like your dental office's Facebook page.

With family, friends, and patients liking your page, you will be well on your way to growing your impact and reach through creating the best Facebook posts on your dental Facebook page and placing the best dental ads for specific promotions and additional reach.

In addition to asking friends, family, and patients to like your page, a great way to get people excited about your practice on Facebook is to create a contest where you hold a random drawing to give away a free treatment to one person who likes your page and then likes, comments, and shares a specific post within a certain timeframe. You could even ask your family, friends, and page fans to nominate someone else to receive the free service.

In my practice, we regularly give back through something we call Project Smile. We do everything on Facebook to reward people who follow our Facebook page, and we don't even tell our patients. The way Project Smile works is we announce we will give away a free smile makeover and ask people to share our announcement post on their Facebook timelines.

The post we ask them to share instructs people to nominate someone who deserves a free smile makeover with an image of their smile, so we can see if they're a candidate. We narrow down the list, invite the finalists for a cleaning to take a closer look at their mouths, and then choose a winner for the full smile makeover. Our Facebook fans love following and sharing our Project Smile posts and often see what other services we provide and come to us for an appointment.

Between invitations, contests, and community-or giving-based promotions, your dental office Facebook page can build a large audience of raving fans for your dental practice.

In the next section, I'll teach you how to draft the best dental practice Facebook posts to build raving fans and loyal patients from Facebook.

How to Create the Best Dental Facebook Posts

Many dentists get overwhelmed by the idea of coming up with content to post to their dental office's Facebook page. The reality is, creating the best dental Facebook posts for your dental practice doesn't have to be complicated. In fact, if you follow two simple rules, your Facebook page can be full of high-impact posts that position you to build deeper relationships with existing fans and patients while attracting new patients into your chair.

How to Know What to Post About

The most important part about creating the *best dental Facebook posts* is to make sure your posts are interesting and engaging. Interesting and engaging posts by a page with likes from family, friends, and patients make it more likely that people will like, comment on, and share your posts. This is important, because the more likes, comments, and shares your Facebook posts get, the more Facebook will show it to other people, and the more chance it has to go viral. Also, people are more likely to like, comment on, or share your dental Facebook post when they see others have liked, commented on, or shared it, especially others they're friends with on Facebook.

To make sure your posts are interesting and engaging to encourage people to like, comment on, or share them, it's important that most of your posts *aren't* promotional offers or even dental tips. Although *some* promotional offers and dental tips are fine, the vast majority of your posts should be about three things:

- Facebook posts showing people your *dental practice's vision* and story to let them know why your dental practice is so great
- Community-oriented Facebook posts, such as events you're participating in or hosting at your practice and other local businesses
- Facebook posts highlighting great things about your team members and patients (with their permission, of course)
- Testimonials from happy patients

These four types of posts help you get people's attention on Facebook, make connections with the right people to grow your dental practice, and encourage people to like, comment on, and share in order to get better reach for your Facebook posts. They also make the promotions and dental tips types of posts get more attention, because Facebook will view your page as one with posts people want to see. Finally, they make it much easier to regularly come up with great fresh content for your page so your dental Facebook page isn't inactive or full of promotional posts.

Creating Facebook Posts about Your Practice Story and Vision

The best dental Facebook posts tell your practice's vision and story so you can let people know why being your patient will be worthwhile. These posts show people the things you're building toward (your vision) and the things you're already doing and have done (your story). These posts humanize your practice and build connections.

In my practice, our vision is to have the best dental practice in the country that treats all our patients like the VIPs they are and delivers WOW experiences to everyone from the moment they walk in until they leave. For example, we provide complimentary gourmet coffees and teas, iPads and noise-canceling headphones to use during an appointment, and hand-and-arm massages by our trained staff to make sure our patients leave feeling more like they just visited a luxury spa than a dentist. We also commit to being active in our community and giving to important causes.

These things are core parts of who we are as a practice, and we want everyone to know it, so we post pictures of our coffees and teas, our patients receiving their relaxing massages (with their permission, of course), of community events, and charitable initiatives. By regularly posting about who we are as a practice, we get many likes, comments, and shares on our posts and build deep relationships with our Facebook fans, because they get to know who we are as a practice and will want their dental-office experience to be like our patients' experiences!

Even if you haven't opened your practice yet, posts about your story and vision for your practice can help connect you with future patients. In fact, one of our dental-marketing clients used this strategy to get hundreds of leads and over fifty appointments scheduled before she even opened!

Creating Community-Oriented Facebook Posts

Posts about events, companies, and people in your community are a great way to become known as a practice that's active and involved in things that matter to your patient pool.

In my practice, we participate in charity runs, host food drives, and have events at our office. We also form strategic alliances with different local businesses each month to offer special deals to their employees. If you do this, you can create a post announcing how excited you are to team up with the business.

Creating Facebook Posts Highlighting Team Members and Patients

Creating Facebook posts that encourage, congratulate, and promote your patients and team members is a great way to highlight people who often go unnoticed. Your team and patients are doing great things in your office and community. Let people know how excited and proud you are about them (with their permission, of course). These posts build deep relationships and get lots of likes, comments, and shares, too!

Posting Patient Testimonials (With Their Permission)

Testimonials from happy patients make great posts. You've earned those testimonials. Make use of them!

Like online reviews, patient testimonials allow other people to boast about why your dental practice is so great, which makes it more likely that people will view it as more trustworthy than if you tell people why your practice is so great.

The Best *Types* of Dental Facebook Posts

Once you know what the best dental Facebook posts are *about*, the next step is to make those posts interesting, varied, and engaging by posting them in different *types* of posts. Generally, you can and should post a variety of text, image, and video Facebook posts to get more attention and engagement without seeming monotonous.

Most dentists are comfortable with text posts, but fewer are comfortable with video and image Facebook posts, so here's how you can use videos and images on your dental Facebook page.

Creating Video Facebook Posts

Video is powerful on Facebook for three important reasons. First, video gets people's attention, especially if their page is set to auto-play. Second, video makes better connections with people once you get their attention, because it invites them into your practice, lets people make virtual eye contact with you, and allows them to hear your voice and see your expressions. Finally, Facebook loves video and will show your post to more people if it has a video.

Video posts on Facebook don't have to be complicated or overproduced. In fact, a good cell-phone camera can be even better than a heavily-produced video, because it seems more authentic and positions you as relatable, not like a stuffy company.

Great uses for video on Facebook posts include Facebook Live video office tours, short recorded video patient testimonials, Facebook Live video Q&A sessions for your patients and the community to ask you what's important to them, Facebook Live or recorded videos of community events, recorded video highlights, and explainer videos with tips about dental insurance, teeth care, new procedures, and more!

Creating Image-Based Facebook Posts
for Your Dental Facebook Page

High-quality image posts get people's attention on Facebook and encourage more engagement than text posts. Some of our favorite ways to use images for my practice and our dental-marketing clients include showing high-quality images of what makes your practice great, like a picture of the iPads we let our patients use and our gourmet-coffee-and-tea station.

Other ways to use image posts with dental Facebook marketing include posting images announcing community events, celebrating patient accomplishments, showing off how great your team is, and highlighting new procedures and equipment.

Like Facebook marketing with videos, marketing with images doesn't need a professional setup. My two rules for creating the best image-based Facebook posts are that a well-lit image you take with a quality cell phone is the best type of picture, and if you can use a picture you take of real patients, team members, and doctors, that is generally better than using a stock image. You can make great impacts with high-quality stock images, but nothing connects with people on Facebook like well-lit, authentic pictures of real people and your real office.

The Best Facebook Ads for Dentists

The real power of Facebook is your ability to post highly targeted Facebook ads. Facebook knows more about its users than almost any other company in the world knows about its customers. They know their income, net worth, location, interests, behavior, family status, age, and more.

For advertisers such as dentists and dental practices, this information is highly valuable, because it allows you to target the right people with your ads and only pay to reach people who are likely to take action on your ad. Here are three important steps for successful Facebook ads for dentists.

Improving Your Dental Facebook Ads by Improving Your Message

First, before placing Facebook ads, be sure each ad has an objective, a goal. Otherwise, you won't know who to target or what to say, and the people who see your Facebook ad are unlikely to take action. Here are eight common goals for dental Facebook ads:

1. Building awareness of your dental practice's culture
2. Showing people what makes your practice different from other practices

3. Talking about your services and how you can help people
4. Highlighting testimonials of happy patients
5. Attracting people into a dental-marketing sales funnel
6. Filling spots left open by last-minute cancelations
7. Promoting a specific procedure
8. Introducing a new dentist or other team member

Once you know the purpose of your Facebook ad, you will have a better understanding of whom to target and what to say to get people to take action to help you achieve your goal.

Improving Your Dental Facebook Ads by Improving Your Targeting

Once you know the goal for your dental Facebook ad, the second step to build a successful Facebook ad campaign is to make sure you target each of your ads to the people who are most likely to resonate with it and take action.

Here are some examples of how to match your Facebook ad targeting to your goals:

- If you want to build awareness of your dental practice's culture, you might not want to target current patients, because they will already know your culture. Instead, you might target an audience Facebook can generate that is similar to your patient population. This is called targeting "lookalike" audiences and is something Facebook can generate automatically if you upload a list of your patients by matching your patients' interests, income, activities, family status, location, and more to those of other Facebook users.
- If you want to fill spots left open by last-minute cancelations, your current patient population is likely going to be your best

bet at achieving your goal, so you might post an ad targeted to only current patients and perhaps offer a free upgraded service or discount to the first person who takes action.

- If you want to advertise dental savings plans, you might consider targeting retired people who no longer have dental insurance.
- If you want to promote a new service, targeting current patients will be more likely to lead to people taking action.
- If you want to get people into a dental-marketing sales funnel, you can target people who have been to your website (called "retargeting" in the Facebook marketing world) with an ad that gives them a call to action to download a free guide or come in for a consultation based on the pages they viewed on your site.

Improving Your Dental Facebook Ads by Choosing the Best Images, Videos, and Copy

Certain words drive people to take action more than others, especially across audiences. The same is true with images and videos. Once you know what you want to accomplish and who you want to target, test different versions of your copy, images, and video. You can do this by creating a split test in Facebook's ad manager.

Split testing Facebook ads is one of the most powerful ways to lower your advertising costs and getting better results, because it's not always possible to know which words, image, or video will resonate at any given time.

Split testing ads is also easier than you might think. In its basic form, to split test a dental ad, all you need to do is create an ad, duplicate the ad, replace the text, image, or video, and submit.

When my team runs dental Facebook advertising campaigns for our dental-marketing clients, we *always* split test the dental Facebook ads we set up. By doing so, we lower costs and get better results. To achieve these results, we set up the split test with a small budget of $3 to $10 per day until we learn which version of the dental Facebook ads is performing the best. Once we choose the winner or winners, we shut off the underperforming ads and let the winners run with an appropriate budget.

Delivering WOW in Action

Dr. Ashley Joves
Smile and Company
Folsom, California
SmileAndCompany.com

After working as an associate for years, I was ready to start my own practice using Delivering WOW to help me build and promote my new startup.

One of the first strategies I put in place was Anissa's teachings on how to use Facebook to grow a dental practice. After my first post went viral, I messaged Anissa to thank her and she has been my personal mentor ever since.

She helped me build my practice Facebook page and use additional Facebook marketing strategies to promote my practice, even as I was still building out my office.

Using her teachings, I had the first three days booked solid, over fifty appointments scheduled altogether, over 1,000 fans on Facebook, and almost 300 people on my practice VIP email list before we even opened the doors.

We achieved this in a community with a dentist to population ratio of 1:660, far lower than the recommended 1:3,000. Even better, we accomplished this using only her dental Facebook strategies and with a marketing budget of just $650.

Additionally, applying Anissa's teachings on team-building, systems, and processes into my practice allowed me to take a week off to go to Hawaii with my family just five months after we opened. Many dentists can't imagine their practice running without them, but my incredible team of Judy, Cynthia, Bianca, and Ashley have my complete trust.

DELIVERING WOW ACTION ACTIVITY:

It's time to start building a WOW Facebook page and marketing campaign. If you haven't set up your dental office's Facebook page yet, go through the steps in this chapter to do so. If you want an interactive guide to this chapter, go to DeliveringWOW.com/Facebook-For-Dentists or the resources page. If you already have a Facebook page for your practice, make sure your Facebook page is complete, professional, and optimized by following the steps in this chapter.

Once your Facebook page is created, invite your family and friends to like your page. Then use the ideas in this chapter to create three Facebook posts this week: one text, one image, and one video, and post them once a day for the next three days.

Finally, I want you to experience the power of Facebook. The best way to take action to experience the power of Facebook ads is to get help, so I created two places to get started for free. First, I built a free Facebook community of over 10,000 dentists all working to build their practices based on my teachings. You can find the link on the resources page or visit us directly at DeliveringWOWHangout.com.

If you're ready to make a commitment to use Facebook to grow your practice, you can also sign up for the Delivering WOW Platinum Coaching Program. In there, you'll get access to my complete Facebook course with videos of me going through the best Facebook strategies. I give you step-by-step guidance and the best and latest Facebook marketing tips, all organized to make it as simple and easy as possible. And you and your team will get coaching from our team of experts in leading and marketing a WOW dental practice.

To join the Delivering WOW Platinum Coaching Program, visit DeliveringWOWPlatinum.com. Once you join, visit the training section, and start the Facebook course. While you're there, be sure to check out the other courses, resources, marketing roadmaps, and free social media images to make posting to Facebook super simple and introduce yourself to the other members in the private forum!

You can also visit DeliveringWOW.com/FB to sign up for my Facebook Bootcamp and receive the latest Facebook marketing training, plug-n-play Facebook ads, a new-patient acquisition funnel you can use with your Facebook ads to attract patients on autopilot, and advanced Facebook support for you and your team!

CHAPTER 11

Ignite Your Passion

Now imagine your new life, your new practice, one with purpose. One where you can choose the lifestyle you wish to live. When you live your purpose, you wake up every day and say, "Wow, I am changing the world!" Make sure to know your purpose. If you don't know what your life's purpose is and how your business can amplify it, that's totally okay. If you don't know your purpose, then your purpose is to find your purpose. It took me a while to come to my purpose, which is to leave a positive impact on everyone that I come in contact with, including my family, my patients, my community, and dentists.

What's your purpose? You might find an answer very quickly, and then you decide no, that's not it. Then you try again. This is a process that you have to develop. But keep asking yourself, and one day you will find that purpose which will be so compelling that it speaks for itself.

Next, find those around you who resonate with your finding that purpose. Start learning from those people how you can better serve them. Once you know your purpose and those whom you want to serve with that purpose, start learning from them. Ask them, and they'll guide you to more success and more wealth.

We recently had a return visit from a patient who first came in two months ago. On her first visit, she shared that she was truly petrified of going to the dentist and told us she might even bite! We just smiled because we knew that she, just like so many other fearful patients, would be transformed. We would WOW her, and her fear would melt away. We told her that at the end of the appointment, she would be so relaxed that she would want not to bite, but to give a hug. We were confident.

We worked with her on easing her anxiety and were confident that she would get the result she desired. We relaxed her with soothing music and the complimentary massage; we took the time to allow her to express her fears. We listened to understand. We provided solutions to her problems and did not judge. Now, things have completely turned around for her. She is no longer petrified. And she has been able to undergo the necessary procedures. In fact, we've now gotten her to a place where she has completed all of her work. Upon her follow-up visit, she said, "Doc, this place is truly amazing."

The essence of the WOW experience is individual care of individual patients each and every time. That's the highest level of customer service. I could not have done that by myself. Getting a win like this goes back to the culture of the place. One of our core values is to deliver a WOW experience every time. That is important to us, and it comes across in how we treat each patient.

We have those wins every single day. When you implement the changes I've discussed in this book and master the Delivering WOW areas I've outlined, you will transform your business. Period. In fact, you and your practice will be respected in the community, and you will have raving fans. You will have team members who love working in your practice, and you will finally get to enjoy your business and your life more.

Remember that story I shared at the beginning of the book, the story of Dr. Scott, the anxious, stressed, and overwhelmed dentist who had no time to attend her child's sporting events and was fighting with her husband over how much time she was spending at work? Her health was taking a beating as her blood pressure was going up, and her work was no longer enjoyable.

Well, that story has changed, after she committed to becoming a Delivering WOW practice. Dr. Scott now is again finding joy in her work. She is working less but bringing in more revenue. She now has time for all the activities that are important to her—including attending her son's ball games, working out, and spending quiet time with her husband. Her marriage is no longer filled with fights and discord. She is off her blood-pressure medication and is planning her big vacation to a dream destination for the next quarter.

What happened? Delivering WOW happened.

While this is a story I created to illustrate the experiences of so many burned-out and stressed-out dentists, the outcome you can experience is real. When you put in place the right systems and team and get the branding down and exemplify the core values and culture that are attractive to your ideal customer, you truly can have a breakthrough. You can have a practice that fulfills your vision and gives you more joy. You can find that you have more time to experience life, more money to give you the freedom you desire, and improved relationships, health, and quality of life.

That is the power of Delivering WOW.

You can change the future of your practice and your life. You can design your future. Business doesn't have to take over your life. You, through your practice, can make a positive contribution to the community. Your practice can have a brand that sets it apart. Struggle can finally be a thing of the past.

You can have patients who love coming to see you, and when they leave, they say, "This was the best dental experience of my life!"

This can be your new WOW reality.

DELIVERING WOW ACTION ACTIVITY:

Write what you have learned about Delivering WOW and how you can apply it to your practice.

CHAPTER 12

Supercharge Your Profitability with High-Growth Marketing Tactics

After putting the foundation of a Delivering WOW practice into place, your next step is to continue to refine your systems and processes to supercharge your profitability, and then pour gas on the fire you've sparked by utilizing more sophisticated marketing techniques that can help your practice make an even greater impact your family, team members, and community.

These are some of the best profit-boosting strategies many of my students and I have used. Before I do, it's important to emphasize that, although I teach many strategies, the truth is you only need to implement a few strategies to build an amazing practice, so choose a few that resonate the best with you and your personality and situation. I include many different options so I can be sure that I include options for any personality. These strategies are designed to give you a handful of complementary strategies to add fuel to your fire once you have the basics in place. They help you set profit goals, set your pricing, make your competition irrelevant, reduce your costs, increase sales, and outsource tasks effectively. Whether you implement them one at a time, or all together, this handful of strategies can make the difference between your struggling just to get by and building a practice that can operate without you.

Reverse Engineering Your Profits

Earlier in the book, I mentioned my whiteboard strategy through which we set targets for each of our services so we could meet daily, monthly, monthly, quarterly, and annual revenue targets. This takes that effort to another level: calculating how much profit you make from each of the services you provide by adding up all the expenses you encounter performing each service, including estimating the amount of time you and your team members spend performing a service, how much supplies you need, and any other costs involved in the service, and then subtracting that from how much revenue you receive for the service on average or by insurance plan. By doing so, you will learn which services to promote in order to maximize the profits of your practice.

Reverse engineering your profits is one of my favorite topics to teach dentists, because it frequently reveals services people are losing money on. If you need help with that, be sure to join our Facebook group or learn more about the Delivering WOW Platinum Coaching Program, where I even share a copy of the Excel template I use to reverse engineer profits in my practice.

Once you know how much profit you make from each service, set goals to maximize the impact of your time in your practice. Maybe you need to raise your price on something, change your insurance relationships, or give up a procedure altogether.

Setting Fees on Margins

After reverse engineering profits for your dental practice, you'll have a list of how much each of the services you perform adds to your bottom line. If you're like many dentists, you'll be surprised to find that some procedures yield higher profits than expected while others yield lower profits than expected—or no profits at all.

If that happens, take some time to consider how you perform each procedure that falls below a desired profit level or profit margin. Can you reduce supply costs for those without sacrificing your practice's culture? Can you delegate activities to reduce team-member costs? Can you increase your price for the service?

Too many dentists set prices based on what other people charge, but other people aren't you. If you're Delivering WOW, you will likely be able to charge a premium for services, because people value the experience with you. Take some time to set fees that allow you to achieve a desired profit margin for each service.

Adding Additional Services to Find Your Blue Ocean

Based on the book, *Blue Ocean Strategy*, by W. Chan Kim and Renée Mauborgne, finding your blue ocean in business terms means designing your business in a way that you create a *new* market so that your traditional competition becomes irrelevant.

When I built my Delivering WOW dental practice, for example, adding things like gourmet teas and coffees, hand-and-arm massages, and iPads almost instantaneously made my practice stand out from other dentists. My practice became the spa-like dental experience, while others were only a place to get your teeth fixed. Since then, we continue to look for opportunities to make our practice stand out. What can you do to find your unique place in the market in a way that attracts patients to your deal?

Negotiating Dental Supplies

While building a dental practice that helps you achieve personal and financial independence, it's important to focus on controlling your costs, and not just marketing and increasing revenue.

Although fixed costs like rent, mortgage, practice debt, and student loans are often locked in for a time, variable costs like dental supply costs can generally be reduced without sacrificing the quality of the services you provide.

One reason for that is because many dental offices don't set budgets or metrics for their dental supplies. Without a budget or metric to measure the cost of supplies, dentists often order too little or too much supplies. This can cause you to run out of supplies needed and be forced to order a small quantity with rush-delivery charges to serve patients. It can also cause supplies to sit too long and expire.

To avoid that, it's important to set a budget for dental supplies as well as a system for ordering them. By controlling your costs and setting a budget for supply costs, you empower yourself to negotiate with your suppliers to lower the costs of supplies that would render the related service unprofitable.

Here are four steps to start controlling your supply costs today.

First, assess how much you spend. If you haven't paid attention to your supply costs, you might be surprised at how high they are. Task a team member with determining how much your practice has spent on dental supplies for the past three months. If this is your first time doing this, you may want to ask them to also determine how much your practice has spent in the past six months and one year to account for any bulk orders you may have made for supplies you're still working through.

Second, compare your supply costs to your revenue for the same time period. When your team member calculates how much you've been spending on dental supplies, compare it to your gross revenue for the same period.

In my practice, we keep our dental costs between five percent and eight percent of our gross revenue. If your percentage is significantly above or below that, consider why that's the case. If your percentage is much higher than eight percent, you could be ordering too much or too little of something, you might need to negotiate, you might need to find an alternative product or distributor, or you might need to reassess whether there's a service that's not profitable for you.

Third, commit to a percentage or amount, and systematize your ordering. When you have a goal and a reason for that goal, it's much easier to change. For example, if your cost for supplies is fifteen percent, you may set a goal to get down to ten percent within two months and between five and eight percent within four months. That gives you motivation to look for ways to reduce those costs as well as a reason and the confidence to ask your team members to press your distributors or suppliers for lower prices or other ways they can help reduce your costs.

Once you know your targets, systematize your ordering so your team knows the budget for supplies and everyone works from one shared spreadsheet or inventory management system to ensure everyone's on the same page. If you're utilizing multiple distributors, you may want to document a process where your team member gets pricing from each distributor and then places an order based on those quotes. You should also make sure you're checking costs on a regular basis, because prices can fluctuate over time, and the source of the best price might not be the same place this year as it was last year.

You can also use a software solution for reducing supply costs, such as Zen Supplies. If you do, make sure to train each of your teammates who will have access to the information.

Finally, evaluate and adjust. As with any new process, it's important that you evaluate your progress on a regular basis and adjust as needed. That can help you improve your costs even more over time and reduce the time you and your team will need to spend on costs. Also, because the costs of specific supplies can vary over time and across suppliers, it's important you don't just find the best option at the beginning and then order that way every time. Remember not to sacrifice quality if quality is one of your core values. It's often possible to reduce costs without sacrificing quality.

Improving Communications to Ensure Patients Accept the Treatment Plans They Need

Before we go into the specific strategy to ensure your patients accept treatment plans they need, it's important to talk about false beliefs that many dentists have about getting patients to accept treatment plans. Many dentists believe that they need to spend a ton of money to get people to come into their practices and accept their treatment plans. The truth is, once you understand how to communicate with your patients, you really don't have to spend a lot of money on expensive ad campaigns to consistently attract new customers, and with a true Delivering WOW practice and cost-effective social marketing campaign, you'll have all the customers and systems you need to build a thriving practice.

In fact, many dentists can achieve their revenue goals by adjusting the way they communicate with their current patients. The assumption that you need to spend a ton of money on marketing and get new patients over and over again to make more money is really not true. In fact, you can virtually *guarantee* that your patients will accept your treatment plans. This is important for dentists whose budgets are tight or who are already busy with patients but whose revenue is stagnant.

The first step to adjusting the way to communicate with your patients is to put yourself in your patients' shoes. Instead of describing the treatment to the patients from a technical perspective, explain it to them in terms of the benefit to them. Be genuine. Be honest. This isn't about tricking people into accepting a treatment plan that they don't need, but in order for the patient to accept the treatment plan, they will need to trust you. Ask yourself, "What does this patient need to believe in order to accept this treatment plan, to want to do that service today?"

I do this exercise with my team all the time, asking them the benefits of each of our services to our patients. This way, our default is to communicate the benefits of the treatments to the patients instead of coming across as *selling* treatments to patients. For example, when I asked my team what a patient who needs sealants might need to believe in order to get sealants done, they gave several answers. One of my team members said they need to understand and believe they're likely to get a cavity without sealants. Another team member said they need to understand it doesn't take a lot of time to do sealants. Another person said they need to believe it's an easy process that doesn't hurt. Thus, instead of saying, "I suggest you get sealants," we shifted our mindset to the patient's perspective and described them as a quick and easy treatment to prevent cavities, which are likely to form without the sealants. From that perspective, the patient knows what they're in for, can make an informed decision, and feels the value proposition.

With a crown, for example, instead of "There's a crack in your tooth, so I think you should get a crown," I emphasize how much of a concern this is by saying, "I'm very concerned about your tooth. There's a crack in your tooth, and your tooth can break at any minute. If that happens, you'll need to have the tooth extracted and a dental implant from an oral surgeon. That process takes six months and can be incredibly expensive.

So, I'm very concerned, and I highly recommend you get a crown immediately." In both cases, I'm telling the patient the truth, but the first way is all about the treatment, and the second way is all about why the treatment is important to them.

Consider the treatments you offer in your office and the benefits to your patients. What bad things do they prevent? What good things do they provide? Consider these things ahead of time so you can communicate your treatment plans to your patients in a way that's focused on their interest. Train your team to do the same. Have brainstorming sessions where you and your team ask each other these same questions. Avoid dental technical babble. That just confuses patients and makes them feel like they're being sold something instead of being advised by a professional who has their best interests in mind. Speak with them in plain language to communicate the benefits and why it's important from the patients' perspectives.

By changing the way you communicate your treatment plans to your patients, you'll virtually guarantee your patients will start accepting the treatment plans they need. Not only will this help you improve your patients' dental health, it will help you increase your revenue without having to spend money on advertising or consistently attract new patients.

Effective Outsourcing

Many dentists read this book, join my Inner Circle Mastermind, or sign up for the Delivering WOW Platinum Coaching Program because they're overwhelmed in their practice and want to make more while working less. If that's you, I want to encourage you. You don't need to implement all of these techniques yourself. Whether you delegate to a team member or outsource to a professional to coach you through the Delivering WOW process or implement many of these tactics, effective outsourcing will help you take back your life. In fact, that's the main reason my team at Delivering WOW now offers many done-for-you services, such as helping dentists run our favorite Facebook marketing campaigns as well as dental-marketing funnels, the final topic I share with you here!

DELIVERING WOW ACTION ACTIVITY:

Choose two of these profit-boosting techniques to implement into your practice over the next two weeks. Also, choose to delegate to a team member or outsource to an outside professional anything that doesn't need your involvement. If you need help outsourcing, email me at connect@deliveringwow.com. I'd be happy to share my favorite connections with you.

CHAPTER 13

Dental-Marketing Funnels, the Secret to Supercharging Your Profits

Every patient of your practice went through the same four steps before becoming your patient. First, they became aware of you.

Second, they became interested in you or something you offered. Third, they decided to interact with you. Fourth, they took action to become your patient.

Typically, this happens either through personal relationships and referrals or through traditional advertising.

When it happens organically through personal relationships and referrals, patients get to know you because of a relationship with you, a team member, friend, or other patient. That relationship causes them to become interested in you or your services, decide to become your patient, and take action to make an appointment and come to your office. Organic practice growth through personal relationships and referrals, while important, only expands your practice to the extent of your ability to build personal relationships with people who refer others or become patients. And we all know our time is limited, which means our time to build relationships is limited.

When it happens through traditional advertising, people get to know you through a paid advertisement on radio, TV, direct mail, phone book, or other traditional way. Generally, these people become interested after repeatedly seeing advertisements or looking for referrals or reading reviews of your practice. They make a decision based on additional interactions with you, often either through more advertising or by calling your office to ask questions about your service or business practices. Finally, after all those advertisements and interactions, they either become a patient or they forget about you.

Traditional Practice Building Is Expensive, Time-consuming, and Ineffective.

If you only attracted new patients with whom you have a personal or referral relationship, your practice would grow very slowly. It would also grow with little patient-demographic control because the common thread across your patients is who they know, not who they are and what services they want.

If everyone beyond a personal and referral relationship required traditional marketing and personal attention, you would spend a lot of time and money attracting people into your patient-acquisition process.

Advertising to people in traditional ways like radio, TV, phone books, direct mail, and newspapers is expensive and inefficient. Even if prospects respond to an ad, you then have to take time away from serving patients to answer questions, follow up, and build relationships with a number of people, many of whom will never become patients. You could pay a team member to do some or all of the intake, but that would be an additional out-of-pocket cost without knowing the return.

Funnels solve all three problems.

Building your practice through funnels is the best way to experience real practice growth. Funnels solve the time and cost problems with traditional practice building, because they get better prospects to you by more effectively targeting prospects, automating and optimizing much of the interest, decision-making, and action-taking processes, and do so at a fraction of the cost. In other words, funnels are better: both more cost-effective and more efficient.

The term *funnel* evokes the visual of the cone-shaped device used to pour liquid into a container. If you picture this tool, the general population of prospects is represented by the space outside the funnel. The top of the funnel represents the process of attracting as many ideal prospects as possible. A little lower into the funnel is the generally smaller number of prospects who become interested. The middle of the funnel contains the even smaller number of people who decide to engage with you. Finally, the smallest part of the funnel represents the people who take action by accepting your offer to become a patient (or to take advantage of a more specific promotion you have offered).

How to Design a High-Performing Funnel for Your Dental Office

Funnels can be created for any number of purposes. For example, you can use a funnel to get people into your office for a specific high-value procedure. You can also use a funnel to build an email list of people to contact if you need to fill a last-minute cancelation. No matter what your goal, you can design a funnel to attract prospects to you and turn them into action takers.

No matter what your goal, here are six thing you need to do to build a basic funnel.

1. Attention: An online post or ad to get the attention of your ideal prospect for the goal of your funnel

Most of the time, this is a Facebook ad that offers something of value to a prospect in order to get them to pay attention. Facebook ads are currently the best and most efficient use of your ad spend, because they're very inexpensive and have the most sophisticated targeting capabilities in the market. That means you can target your ad to a group of your ideal prospects for less money than you would spend on less-targeted ads.

For example, you can target existing patients. You can target people whom Facebook knows to be like your existing patients or like people who interact with your Facebook page, which is known as a lookalike audience. The options are almost endless.

For example, you may want to promote teeth whitening to a lookalike audience of your patients with the goal of getting new long-term patients by offering fifty percent off teeth whitening when someone books a cleaning by a certain date. We did this with someone in my Inner Circle Mastermind, who saw great engagement.

Your ad has one goal: to get a prospect to notice you and click on a link in the ad, which will automatically send them to the next part of your funnel, which is your squeeze page or landing page.

2. A squeeze page or landing page

A squeeze page or landing page is a single page on a website designed to collect contact information from a prospect, otherwise called "opting in" to your offer. It then triggers the next step of your funnel.

This is often done with squeeze-page software like ClickFunnels, which makes it easy to set up landing pages to collect information and trigger the next part of your funnel, delivering on your ad's promise.

3. Delivering on your ad's promise for people who opt in on your landing page

When people opt in on your landing page, the next step is to deliver on your ad's promise. Depending on your funnel's goal, the next step might be to automatically email the prospect a checklist or guide, a link to a video you recorded, a sequence of messages answering common questions about a procedure, a promised coupon, or even an appointment scheduler.

Using simple-but-sophisticated software like ClickFunnels makes this easy, but no matter what software you use, once someone opts into your squeeze page or landing page by giving you their contact information, the next step is to deliver on your ad's promise.

4. Reconnecting with (or retargeting) people who don't opt in on your landing page

When people click on the link in your ad but don't opt in on your landing page, chances are they were initially interested in your offer but either lost interest or got distracted. This is natural; it often takes multiple touches to attract people's attention and get them to accept an offer. In fact, the typical landing page only collects information between ten and twenty percent of the time.

Because of that, the best practice is to use another ad to target the people who click on the first ad but don't opt in on the landing page. This second ad is often a reminder to take advantage of the offer that appeared in the first ad.

This is called "retargeting" and is simple to set up with Facebook and software like ClickFunnels. Essentially, the way this works is you place on your landing page a small piece of code that Facebook provides. The code gets read by Facebook and tells you who landed on your squeeze page but not your confirmation or thank-you page.

You then target that group of people with a new ad. The new ad acts similarly to the initial ad, asking them to click a link to land on your squeeze page, where you again ask them to opt in.

5. Asking your prospects to take action

Once someone opts in and you deliver on your ad's promise for a guide, coupon, or other piece of value, your funnel software will email them to complete the patient-acquisition process.

For a simple goal such as getting people to come in for a cleaning and teeth whitening, you could ask them to take action in the email where you deliver the coupon. For more complicated or higher-ticket items such as dental implants, before asking them to make an appointment, you might send them a number of emails introducing them to your practice, answering frequently asked questions, and delivering a video where you compare the differences between a bridge and implants.

6. Retargeting those who opt in but don't take action to become patients

The best funnels are the ones that build on themselves based on the actions of your prospects. One way to make sure your funnel works for you is to export a list of people who made it to the end of your funnel but didn't take action and send them a different sequence of emails to build a deeper relationship with them and retarget them with Facebook ads to stay top of mind and encourage them to take action.

3 Types of Marketing Funnels to Implement in Your Dental Office

To get you started, here are three types of marketing funnels you can add to your dental-marketing plan to help you skyrocket your profits and patient numbers.

1. Funnels Designed to Sell Additional Existing Services to Current Patients

One of the easiest ways to increase your profitability is through offering additional services to current patients. This is because you've already broken down the four biggest barriers to business with them, including getting them to know, like, and trust you; and they have already paid you money either directly or through their insurance plan. With those four barriers broken down, you don't have to worry as much about getting their attention and convincing them that you're trustworthy and likable enough for them to do business with you.

The only barriers you'll have to break down through your funnel is the barriers they have with additional services that can benefit them.

To implement this type of funnel, first follow this process for building a dental-marketing funnel. Once you have that funnel set up, with a high-value piece of opt-in content, you can reach out to your current patients in whatever way you typically get the most engagement to get them to go to your squeeze page and opt in.

In many cases, this will be by email or a Facebook ad or event targeted to your patient list, but it doesn't have to be. If your patients respond best to text messages or Facebook Messenger bots, send messages there letting them know you have a great free piece of information about the service you'd like to promote with a link to your squeeze page.

2. Funnels Designed to Introduce
New Services to Current Patients

Another great way to grow your dental practice is to add new, high-profit services to your procedure mix and offer them to your current patients. Dental-marketing funnels are a great way to gauge interest in new procedures and even pre-book appointments without investing thousands of dollars or hundreds of hours building a traditional marketing plan.

Not only are funnels more effective and affordable than traditional marketing, they can be tweaked and evaluated instantaneously with sophisticated statistics to let you know what's working and what's not. It can even save you time and money by helping you test the appetite for specific procedures before investing significant time or money incorporating them into your practice.

To implement this type of funnel, all you need to do to is build your funnel for the procedure you're considering adding and send your patients to your squeeze page to opt in, just like with the first funnel strategy for selling additional existing services.

3. Funnels Designed to Attract New Patients

If your practice already has a robust procedure offering and high-revenue patients, a funnel to attract new patients into your practice might be the right next move.

One way to design this funnel is to present an offer, such as a half-priced whitening procedure, to anyone who comes in for a cleaning, and then introduce your practice to them in the funnel to build a relationship with them and show them why they should choose you as their dentist. By using a funnel to build a relationship with them instead of just letting them download a coupon, you can help reduce the risk that people who take advantage of the offer will come in just for the one service and move on.

Another way to design this funnel is to promote a specific procedure like dental implants or Invisalign. With these types of funnels, you can attract patients for a high-value service and nurture the relationship in the funnel and by serving them well when you perform the procedure.

Simplifying Dental-Marketing funnels

Many dentists avoid or delay using dental-marketing funnels, sticking to old, expensive, inefficient dental-marketing tactics, because those old tactics are familiar to them or because they think dental-marketing funnels aren't a good fit for them or their practice.

I've heard every objection imaginable, but after helping thousands of dentists grow their practices, I'm more convinced than ever that *every* dentist can implement a dental-marketing funnel into their practice to make their marketing easier. Here are three common misconceptions about dental-marketing funnels.

1. They're only for existing practices.

Although dental-marketing funnels are cheaper, automated, and more effective, there's not much of a difference between them and traditional marketing methods with respect to what type of practice can benefit from a funnel.

In fact, one of my clients, Dr. Ashley Joves, who is featured in the Delivering WOW in Action section at the end of Chapter 10, didn't even *have* a practice when she got started, and by the time she opened the doors, she had over 1,000 Facebook fans, almost 300 people on her Very Important Patient email list, and over 50 appointments booked.

It doesn't matter if you've been in business 40 years or 40 seconds, or if you're still 40 days away from opening your doors; dental-marketing funnels can help you grow.

2. They're complicated.

Mistakenly assuming dental-marketing funnels are complicated is a common error. The truth is funnels *can* be complicated, but they don't need to be. They *can* be a multi-step, sophisticated series of emails that adapt to what each subscriber does based on internal email links that act as triggers for different email sequences. All of that's *possible*.

But they *don't have to be* complicated. In fact, the technology Dr. Joves used to get almost 300 people on her VIP wait list and have over 50 people schedule appointments before she even opened the doors involved two simple steps: (1) setting up a squeeze page in ClickFunnels for people to enter their name and email address, and (2) an automated email delivering a coupon to them. Everything else was done on Facebook and by sending emails to her growing list.

3. They're hard to set up.

If you have *any* experience managing patient contact information for emails or direct mail, you or your team can set up a funnel. Software like ClickFunnels makes it super easy, with a visual workflow approach and drag-and-drop technology to set up your pages. ClickFunnels makes setting up your funnel simple.

To get the most out of your funnel, I recommend either working with experienced funnel experts to help you design the best funnel for your goals or working from a marketing-funnel template that's known to have worked for others. My team and I offer several marketing-funnel templates to our clients and students for free! We have helped a number of dentists implement funnels in their practice and love celebrating with each of them as their practice starts to grow and would love to help you do the same!

Building Your First Dental-Marketing Funnel

Now that I've shared why every practice needs a funnel, three types of funnels you can implement in your practice, and three misconceptions about dental-marketing funnels, it's time for you to take action and build your first marketing funnel for your practice!

Follow these six steps, and you can have your first dental-marketing funnel and get it live and working to turn strangers into patients this week!

1. Set a goal for your funnel.

For this example, we're going to use Invisalign as the procedure we're looking to promote with a funnel. The goal for this funnel will be to get more people to come to you for Invisalign treatment.

2. Create targeted, high-value opt-in content.

Create a short piece of content that will help and attract your ideal funnel target. The more connected this checklist or guide is to the goal, the better, because the goal is to get people who fit your goal into the funnel and exclude everyone else.

For example, doing a drawing for a free iPad would attract everyone, and you'll end up with a list of people that have no connection to the goal. On the other hand, offering a checklist for people to find out if they're a candidate for Invisalign, or a guide that answers the most frequently asked questions about Invisalign would attract people who are considering Invisalign and not attract anyone else. In this case, we'll use the checklist to find out if someone's a candidate for Invisalign as the content.

3. Schedule a Facebook Live event to attract people into your funnel.

For this example, I suggest scheduling a Facebook Live Q&A Session about Invisalign, because it's a simple event that requires very little preparation. That makes it a great option for your first dental-marketing funnel. All you need to do is show up and answer the questions you normally answer from people in your chair. This Facebook Live is designed to get the attention of people who have considered Invisalign but who haven't followed through to get Invisalign treatments.

Promote your upcoming Live Event for the two days before the event, letting people know you'll be doing a live Q&A session right on Facebook answering any and all questions they have about Invisalign. Promote the event to your Facebook fans, patients, and any other relevant audiences. Send an email to your patient list letting them know about the upcoming Live Event and, if you have a Facebook Messenger bot set up, let them know there as well. During the live Q&A session, give people a call to action to go to a separate page to sign up for the checklist to find out if they're a candidate for Invisalign. I suggest using *ClickFunnels* for this. You can find my recommended Facebook Messenger bot companies and a link to receive a free trial to ClickFunnels on the resources page.

On the thank-you page, which is the page they will see once they sign up, create a button that takes them to a page on your website, where you have before-and-after pictures of Invisalign patients. Deliver the checklist through an introductory email.

Make sure to put a Facebook pixel on the opt-in page and thank-you page so if they don't opt in, you show them a different ad that reminds them to take up the PDF and get the promotion.

4. Promote the event replay to get more people into your funnel.
After you record the live Q&A session, spend an additional $50 on Facebook ads for the video, targeting your patients, past website visitors, people who have engaged with your page, or a Facebook-matched lookalike audience. This will put your video in their feeds. After two

days, invest more money continuing to run the ads that are performing well. Stop the ads that aren't performing well. For example, if the website visitors ad is performing well but the lookalike audience isn't, stop the ad targeted to the lookalike audience and invest more into targeting past website visitors.

5. Create a relationship-building email sequence with a call to action.

In this case, I suggest a five-day nurture email sequence, as follows.

Day 1: When they sign up, immediately send them the checklist with the following email:

Subject: Here's Your Invisalign Checklist

Content (to personalize): Thanks for signing up for the Invisalign Checklist! Invisalign provides patients with an opportunity to [insert the benefit you want to promote]. To tell you a little more about our practice, [insert a brief description about what makes your practice special].

We also want to give you a thank-you gift for taking action, which is an offer to save [insert a discount] off your Invisalign Treatment, good any time in the next six weeks!

We can't wait to meet you!

Day 2: Subject: How Invisalign Changed [Suzi's] Life

Content: Share a story of a happy Invisalign patient. Even better: add a testimonial video if you can.

Day 3: Subject: Why we serve

Content: Share a short story of why your practice serves people, why you went into dentistry, or what makes your practice unique.

Day 4: Subject: Our Guarantee to You as a VIP Patient

Content: Be bold. Make a guarantee for them. For my practice, we let people know we guarantee on-time appointments, peace of mind, and WOW experiences.

Day 5: Subject We've Got Something Special for YOU!

Content: Recap who you are, why you serve, the benefits of Invisalign, and how Invisalign changed [Suzi's] life, and then give them call to action to come in for Invisalign. Reiterate the discount.

6. Review, revise, and repeat the process.

As with anything, you will find places to improve your funnel. Pay attention to what can be improved, make the improvements, and repeat the process. For example, you might swap out testimonial videos, change the thank-you gift, or re-record the live Q&A. Improve what you can, then continue running the promotion to get people to opt in to your email sequence.

3 Ways to Get More People into Your Dental-Marketing Funnel

As effective as funnels can be, even the best-planned automated sequence won't help you grow your practice if you aren't attracting enough of the right people into the funnel.

Here are three ways to attract more of the right people into your dental-marketing funnel, so your automated sequence can guide them to your call to action.

1. Create and promote high-value opt-in content.

Creating a piece of high-value opt-in content is the second step in setting up your funnel, because high-value opt-in content such as guides, checklists, eBooks, explainer videos, or answers to frequently asked questions has been proven to attract people to your funnel, giving them useful information in exchange for their contact information.

Although it's important to create high-value opt-in content while you build your funnel, that doesn't mean you can forget about opt-in content after you create it. To attract more people into your funnel, consider creating multiple pieces of high-value opt-in content for each funnel. For example, you might have a short checklist, pre-recorded video, and a pre-recorded audio interview that align with the goal of your funnel.

Having multiple pieces of high-value opt-in content allows you to attract more people into your funnel, because different people have different preferences. Some people prefer video. Others prefer audio. Others will only consume written content. Also, creating multiple pieces of content on related but slightly different topics helps you connect with people using multiple messages.

2. Create and recreate multiple Facebook Live events.

Promoting *replays* of live events is a great way to leverage your time to attract people into your funnel without having to spend additional time doing the same Facebook Live events, on the same topic, multiple time. Thus, promoting replays frees your time up to do different types events of events on the same topic, such as a live demonstration followed by a live Q&A on another day, and then promote both replays. It also allows you to do multiple events on different topics, so you can test and run many promotions at once. If you're not attracting as many people to your funnel as you want, consider creating multiple Facebook Live events to lead people into your funnel.

The more Facebook Live events you do, the more comfortable you'll get with them, and the more effective you will be at leading people to download your opt-in content to get them into your funnel. Thus, consider recreating the same Facebook Live events as you get more comfortable with live video and sending people to your opt-in. You can also experiment with hosting Facebook Live events at different times of the day to see if one time is more effective than another.

Finally, as with the opt-in content, you could host Facebook Live events on slightly different topics until you find one that works better than others. By creating and recreating multiple Facebook Live events, you'll have more touches with people live, better content as you become more comfortable with live video, and multiple video replays to boost on Facebook and promote to your email list.

3. Promote your opt-in content to your patient email list.
If the goal of your funnel is to sell a specific service, rather than to attract new patients to your practice, your existing patient list can be a great place to go to get more people into your funnel.

Because your current patients already know, like, and trust you, they can be much more open to opting in to your funnel for additional services than others who don't know how great you and your practice are!

Thus, emailing them to let them know about your great new opt-in content or event with a link to your squeeze page can be highly effective at attracting people into your funnel!

How to Spot and Plug any Leaks
in Your Dental-Marketing Funnel
Like any onboarding or sales process, the more qualified leads you get into and through your funnel, the better your results will be! But what if you did everything right, set up your funnel, and the leads aren't coming? Your marketing funnel might have a leak! Don't worry, it

happens. The more funnels you build, the better they will work. And the longer each funnel is in place, the more you'll learn about it and how to improve it. Here are three ways to spot and plug common leaks in your funnel.

Unqualified People Are Making It into Your Funnel

A good marketing funnel is designed with a goal in mind. Your goal might be to acquire a new patient, offer a new service to existing patients, or to promote an existing procedure. Whatever it is, your funnel needs to attract people who are a good match for the goal and offer a piece of targeted, high-value opt-in content to get their attention and get them to opt in to your funnel sequence.

If you notice a number of unqualified people making it into your funnel, it's likely because something isn't targeted enough. Either your opt-in content isn't targeted enough, or your efforts to attract people into your funnel (like Facebook ads) aren't targeted enough.

For example, if you're looking to attract people into an automated Invisalign marketing funnel, opt-in content about teeth whitening would likely attract a number of people who would not be interested in Invisalign. On the other hand, content that answers frequently asked questions about Invisalign or shares how to know if you qualify for Invisalign would *only* attract people who are interested in Invisalign.

If your opt-in content is targeted and high-value content, and you're still seeing unqualified people getting into your funnel who shouldn't be, such as people from outside your service area, it's possible your outreach isn't targeted enough. For example, your Facebook ads audience might need to be adjusted by location to your area to make sure you're only paying for clicks from people who are interested in your service and likely to come to *you* if they decide your offer is for them.

People Getting Stuck in Your Funnel

If you're getting mostly qualified leads into your funnel, but people aren't making it all the way through your funnel, take a close look at the part of your funnel they tend to get stuck at. Does it deliver on the promise from the previous step? Is it off topic? Does it skip too far ahead of the step before it? Does that step encourage people to move to the next step?

Adjust the step where people are getting stuck to make sure it delivers a promise from the previous step, is a logical next step from the last step in the onboarding or sales process, delivers a promise, and gives another reason for your ideal prospects to move to the next step of your funnel.

People Who Aren't Ready to Take the Next Step at the End of Your Funnel

If your funnel is attracting qualified people and leading them through the end, but they're still not taking action, it's possible you have an incomplete funnel. In this case, it's likely that you've presented your funnel well to attract qualified leads and offered valuable content to them each next step along the way. The issue is likely that:

- Your call to action is too big a step from where your funnel ends,
- Your funnel doesn't address at least one question prospects typically have, or
- You haven't built trust and rapport into your funnel.

Take a look at your funnel process with your ideal prospect in mind. Is your call to action too big a step from the end of your funnel? Are there additional questions you need to answer? Did you build enough trust and rapport with them so they get to know, like, and trust *you* and don't just take your info and go somewhere else?

Lowering Your Costs and Getting Even More People into Your Dental-Marketing Funnel

Even if you've developed a high-performing, leak-free funnel, you can still improve your results and lower your costs by optimizing the way you attract people into your funnel.

The best way we've found to attract people into your funnel is through targeted Facebook ads that send people to a page that exchanges a highly relevant guide or promotion to people in exchange for their contact information.

The most basic form of Facebook ad that gets people into your funnel is a simple post presenting your guide or offer. Although the technique is predictably effective, results can vary from time to time, even if you use exactly the same text, image, and audience—for two reasons.

First, people are often unpredictable. What works in one demographic might not work in another. What works one day might not work another. Also, people tend to act in groups, so if one ad gets many likes, shares, or comments, then others will join in, even if another ad has better copy or imagery.

Second, Facebook's algorithm is set to build momentum in similar ways in order to ensure their members are shown the most relevant ads. Thus, Facebook will give more exposure to ads that get more engagement and even do so at lower costs than for posts with lower engagement.

Thus, the most effective Facebook ads take advantage of both human behavior and Facebook algorithm tendencies in order to reduce costs and increase results and that's why it's best to split test Facebook ads, like we talked about in Chapter 10.

The same is true with the Facebook ads you place to lead people to your dental-marketing funnels. It's impossible to predict which organic or paid posts will get the most engagement and better results, so you test both. With organic posting, it's best to try different types of posts between live video, recorded video, images, etc. With Facebook ads, duplicating ads and making minimal changes to each element until you find the best ad for your goal can lower your costs to get people to your funnel and improve your results.

With traditional marketing, split testing is expensive and difficult to do because you need to either print multiple versions of the same physical mailer or place multiple ads in different newspapers, television programs, or phone books. It's also difficult to quickly get reliable statistics or run ads without spending hundreds if not thousands of dollars setting it up plus the time it takes to identify the best traditional opportunities and negotiate the best rates and ad placement.

With Facebook marketing and dental-marketing funnels, split testing is super quick and easy and can be done with a few clicks. Even better, you can get reliable data in a matter of a few days for just a few dollars, and your ads go live within minutes of your submitting it—for the best price with no searching or negotiating rates or placement.

For these reasons, the most successful dental marketers utilize optimized dental-marketing funnels with Facebook ads and conduct split tests of every Facebook ad they post to get the best results at the lowest cost. Here's how to split test your Facebook ads, so you can get more people into your funnel while lowering your costs, too.

Set up your Facebook ad split test.

The first step of a split test is to simply set up a Facebook ad like normal. We recommend setting a budget of between $3 and $10 for the ad. That's plenty of money to get reliable data.

Once you have your Facebook ad set up, you need to duplicate the ad. You can choose as many copies of the original as you would like and keep your budget for each ad the same as the original. For our dental-marketing clients, we choose one, two, or three copies; our clients have between two and four versions of the same ad running at any time. In some cases, we have up to eight versions of the same ad running.

Once you've duplicated the ad, edit each of the ads to change one element. The most frequently-changed and tested elements include the headline, copy, images, audience, or the offer itself. For example, you might send two ads to the same audience, with one offering a free guide and the other offering a deal, to see which converts better. You can also test two, three, or even four different images with the same audience and ad copy to see which one resonates better. You can even test two different audiences with the same elements. We recommend keeping it simple when you're starting out or outsourcing your Facebook ads to an experienced ads manager to help you, as our dental-marketing clients do by outsourcing to me and my team.

Evaluate your Facebook ad split test.

Split testing your Facebook ads can push even your best-performing funnels to new levels, so I encourage people to keep testing if they want to keep improving their results. Imagine setting up a split test and discovering your *original* ad performed at double or triple the cost of your other versions and attracted fewer people. Had you not split tested, you'd be stuck with those results. With split testing, you can click one button after spending less than $10 on a $3-per-day budget and let the other versions continue to perform at levels your original ad couldn't touch.

To evaluate your split tests, check the performance after a few days by going back into Facebook Ads Manager or Power Editor and checking how each ad is performing. You may find that all ads are working well, producing similar, great results. In that case, you might choose not to change anything. You may also find that one or two versions are performing at significantly higher costs than the others or attracting significantly fewer leads. In that case, with one click, simply shut off each one that isn't doing well, and let the ones that are performing best keep going. It's that easy!

Split test your funnel in ClickFunnels.
In addition to split testing your Facebook ads, ClickFunnels allows you to split test each step of your funnel itself, so you can achieve the best performance for each step of your funnel. Split testing in ClickFunnels is even easier than with Facebook ads and can be done in a few clicks. All you need to do is go to the funnel you want to split test, click "Start Split Test," create a variation of your existing funnel, edit the variation, similar to how you'd do with Facebook, and click the "Start Split Test" button.

ClickFunnels will then run both versions of the funnel and let you know how they're performing. You can pause, edit, or stop the split test whenever you want. Once you have enough traffic to your funnel to see which version performs the best, you can declare the winner and use the best-performing version.

The most successful marketers constantly test and improve their marketing. You might not want to fix what isn't broken, but that doesn't mean you can't improve it! That's what split testing allows you to do.

When we split test for our clients in their Facebook Ads Manager and ClickFunnels accounts, we often find the first version of an ad or landing page isn't the best-performing one, even if it performs well within goals and expectations. Because of that, we split test everything in order to continually improve results. I highly recommend you split test even your best-performing funnels in order to get the best results you can with your marketing time, effort, and budget.

If you're having trouble optimizing your already-performing dental-marketing funnels, consider split testing in Facebook Ads Manager or ClickFunnels.

DELIVERING WOW ACTION ACTIVITY:

Because an effective automated funnel cuts your intake time down to nearly nothing, getting people into an automated dental-marketing funnel is one of the best uses of your marketing time. Consider three ways you can use funnels to automate some of the marketing or intake activities in your practice. Decide to implement at least one funnel this month, either by doing it yourself or outsourcing to a professional. If you need help or have any questions, join the free Facebook community or connect with my team and me. We regularly build funnels for my practice and other dentists and dental practices and would be happy to answer any questions you have! You can connect with us at Connect@DeliveringWOW.com.

Additionally, the Delivering WOW Platinum Coaching Program has a full Funnel Mastery Course with videos of me going through the latest and best dental-marketing funnel strategies. I give you step-by-step guidance all organized to make funnels as simple and easy as possible.

To join the Delivering WOW Platinum Coaching Program, visit DeliveringWOWPlatinum.com. Again, while you're there, be sure to check out the other courses, resources, marketing roadmaps, and free social media images, and introduce yourself to the other members in the private forum!

You can also visit DeliveringWOW.com/FB to sign up for my Facebook Bootcamp. In addition to all the Facebook training, support, and other benefits, Facebook Bootcamp members receive a copy of my actual automated patient-acquisition funnel they can use with Facebook ads to attract patients on autopilot.

CHAPTER 14

Moving Forward

Purpose, passion, and persistence. These make up the secret sauce to success. No business grows consistently. There will always be times of struggle. You have to be consistent. Once you have a purpose, discover your passion. Once you discover your passion, you will be excited. You will know that what you provide will benefit people. Then it's all about the transfer of that energy. Dentistry is not about fixing or repairing teeth. It's about the end benefits of what solutions you are providing. It's about changing lives.

It's about the benefits you can transfer. The best dentists realize that what's most important is the end benefit. You are giving someone confidence to go after that new job. You are giving someone better health because their gums won't get a disease. You are giving someone longevity in life. You are giving someone a job, so they can now achieve their life's passion. When you discover this, then creating a fascinating practice will be easy.

My goal in writing this book is to inspire dentists along their journey to think out of the box. You don't have to accept the status quo as an unshakable reality. You don't have to feel stuck in your practice, stressed out, and receiving no real joy. No, you can create a WOW practice and have an extraordinary business with massive growth.

You've got the plan. Now, it's up to you. What will you do now? Will you continue in the same way, or will you take what you've learned here and get going on creating WOW in your business? There is no need to be scared or intimidated or to believe that it's too late for you: It doesn't matter how long you've been in business, because Delivering WOW isn't about where you start. It's about where you can finish.

You don't have to continue slogging away, thinking it will take you twenty years or more to get to a good place. You can get to a WOW place now. Growing your business isn't about what you do someday. It's about what you choose to do now, starting today.

I invite you to be a part of the Delivering WOW experience. Start now by taking your practice and your life to the next level. I've pointed you in the direction, but this book is just the start. You will have more to learn so you can dive deeper. If you know you want to, for example, master today's top marketing strategy of social media, then commit to a course. Get a coach. Join a mastermind or an online community of like-minded dentists who will stretch you and hold you accountable.

I continue to learn, and my mastermind partners help to keep me focused. Your vision, too, will involve many others. Be prepared to get them excited and engaged to take the journey with you.

It's all about action.

One caution, though, as you go forward: Learning is great. Wonderful. But the transformation you seek will not happen without action. So, don't just read what I've written. Act upon it. Anything you want to improve is something you need to focus on. If you want to have more profits in your business, you need to focus on all steps that make up profits. If you want to work fewer days a week, then put the steps in place to make that happen. If you want to take a trip, book the ticket.

If your aim is to create a WOW dental practice, then write what you want, put in place the steps, and take action!

Remember:

- Write the vision. Be specific. Engage others in your vision and get them excited about supporting it.
- Identify your culture. Determine the type of company culture you need that will help you move toward your vision. What story will you tell the world about your practice?
- Focus on the set of core values that set the tone around the practice. Live your core values and make them the heart of your practice.
- Hire and train the right team. Invest in your team's professional development and learning. Be open to your team, listen to them, and encourage them to see themselves in your vision. Delegate, automate, or eliminate tasks that take you away from doing what you do best in your business.
- Implement systems for the repeatable activities you engage in. Write all of the steps for every process in your practice, and review twice a year to ensure that all stays current.
- Share your brand through strategic marketing so you attract your ideal customers. Put in place social media marketing, as

well as some of the other marketing strategies discussed in the book. Always test and measure.

Get help.

You don't need to do this alone. Since releasing the first edition of this book, I've connected with thousands of dentists, creating communities, courses, and bootcamps to help you walk through the Delivering WOW process. Whether you're just getting started or have implemented the Delivering WOW experience into your practice and now want to increase revenue and profits through the more sophisticated techniques, having mentorship and support is key.

I'd be honored to help you. You can get started by listening to my Delivering WOW Dental Podcast on iTunes, visiting my website at DeliveringWOW.com for my latest articles and free resources, or joining me and thousands of other dentists in the free Dental Marketing and Profits Facebook group by visiting DentalMarketingAndProfits.com.

If you're serious taking massive action to take control of your business and personal life and building the practice of your dreams, then join me in the Delivering WOW Platinum Coaching Program by going to DeliveringWOWPlatinum.com or sign up for my next 21-Day Marketing and Practice Growth Challenge, which you can read about at DeliveringWOWChallenge.com.

The step-by-step training in the Delivering WOW Platinum Coaching Program covers:

- Facebook for dentists
- Facebook marketing for dental offices
- Email marketing for dentists
- Online reviews for dentists
- Dental office SEO
- Facebook Messenger bots marketing
- How to create a twelve-month marketing plan

- How to create an in-house dental plan
- How to set up strategic alliances
- How to recruit and train a R-O-C-K-S-T-A-R team
- How to get your TEAM aligned to your vision
- How to create consistent systems and KPI's
- How to get your patients to say "YES"
- How to reverse engineer your production goals
- How to set your fees based on margins
- How to save on dental supplies
- How to decrease overhead
- How to create a practice that can run without you
- And more!

The Delivering WOW Platinum Coaching Program also includes private forums to get advice and feedback from me, my team, and other members, free social media images to share on your channels and make your social media marketing even easier, and a roadmap to walk you through building your dream practice!

If you're ready to get started building the best dental practice with the best dental marketing, please do! Visit DeliveringWOWPlatinum.com to learn how the Delivering WOW Platinum Coaching Program can help you build a Delivering WOW practice!

You can also join my free Dental Marketing and Profits Facebook group, where thousands of dentists and I help each other build better practices. You can find the link to join on the resources page or go straight to DentalMarketingAndProfits.com.

Don't forget to grab all the resources I mentioned on the resources page: DeliveringWOW.com/WOWResources.

You're ready.

Dream big and have fun.

Now go and start Delivering WOW!

About the Author

Dr. Anissa Holmes has been voted one of the Top 25 Women in Dentistry by Dental Products Report and has the leading dental practice for Delivering WOW in Jamaica.

A social media strategist, author, speaker, podcaster, and practicing dentist, she shows dentists how to create profitable and thriving businesses and has built a team to provide done-for-you marketing services.

She is a graduate of the University of Alabama School of Dentistry and lives in Jamaica with her husband and two children.

She loves to hear from readers. Here's how you can connect with Anissa today.

Join the Delivering WOW Platinum Coaching Program at DeliveringWOWPlatinum.com.

Sign up for her next 21-Day Marketing and Practice Growth Challenges at DeliveringWOWChallenge.com.

Join the free Dental Marketing and Profits Facebook group at DentalMarketingAndProfits.com.

Sign up for the Facebook Bootcamp at DeliveringWOW.com/FB to get the latest Facebook marketing training, plug-n-play Facebook ads, a new-patient acquisition funnel you can use with your Facebook ads to attract patients on autopilot, and advanced Facebook support for you and your team.

Visit her website at DeliveringWOW.com.

Like her practice Facebook page at Facebook.com/JamaicaSmiles.

Subscribe to her Delivering WOW Dental Podcast on iTunes at DeliveringWOW.com/iTunes.